Should you do it yourself?
Should you hire a contractor?
Should you divide the work between yourself
and a professional?

Do-It-Yourself . . . or Not? is the only reference guide you'll need to answer these and most other common questions about basic home improvement. Easy to use, *Do-It-Yourself . . . or Not?* can teach you how to replace or install almost anything in your home—even if you've never considered yourself handy. It provides simple directions for completing 100 common household tasks, as well as information on renting special tools, finding a good contractor, and determining how much time and money it will take to get the job done right.

The authors of a popular syndicated newspaper column on home improvements, Katie and Gene Hamilton are experts on teaching ordinary people how to make their homes everything they want them to be. So avoid expensive errors and time-wasting tactics: Let the Hamiltons show you if you should do it yourself . . . or not!

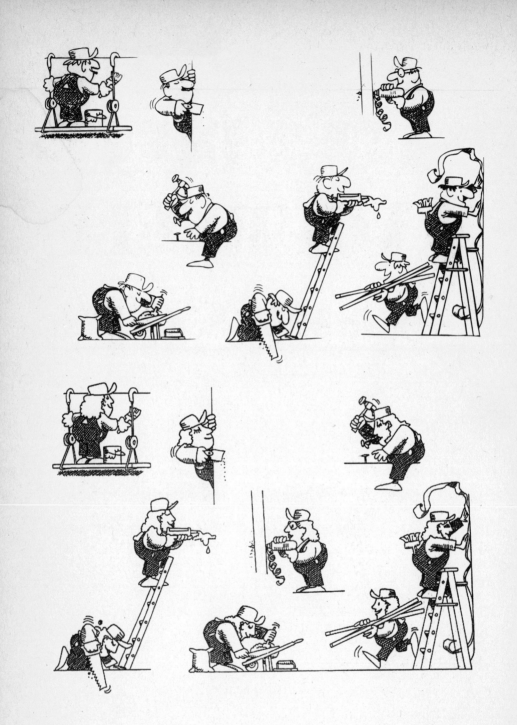

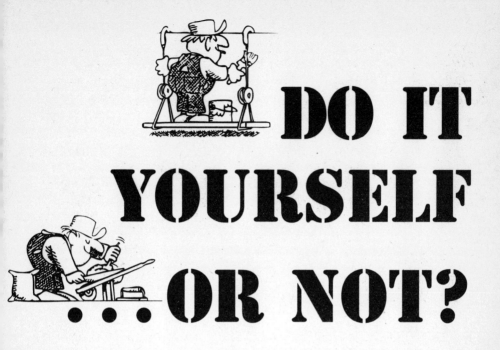

DO IT YOURSELF ...OR NOT?

KATIE AND GENE HAMILTON

BERKLEY BOOKS, NEW YORK

DO IT YOURSELF . . . OR NOT?

A Berkley Book / published by arrangement with
A Perfect Partnership

PRINTING HISTORY
Berkley trade paperback edition / February 1996

ISBN: 0-425-15202-2

BERKLEY®
Berkley Books are published by The Berkley Publishing Group,
200 Madison Avenue, New York, New York 10016.
BERKLEY and the "B" design
are trademarks belonging to Berkley Publishing Corporation.

PRINTED IN THE UNITED STATES OF AMERICA

10 9 8 7 6 5 4 3 2 1

CONTENTS

INTRODUCTION 1

CHAPTER 1
Remove Wallpaper 3 • Refinish a Hardwood Floor 5 • Install Carpeting 6 • Add Polystyrene Molding to Trim Out a Room 8 • Paint a Room 9 • Texture a Ceiling 11 • Install Interior Window Shutters 12 • Wallpaper a Room 14 • Install Vertical Blinds on a Patio Door 15 • Build and Upholster a Window Cornice Board 17 • Install Paneling 18 • Wainscot a Room 20 • Paint a Wooden Floor 21

CHAPTER 2
Install Quarry Tile in a Mudroom 23 • Install a Pet Door 25 • Install Prefinished Plank Wood Flooring 26 • Install Fold-Away Attic Stairs 27 • Install a Suspended Ceiling 29 • Install a Sliding Tub Door 30 • Install Ceramic Tile on Bathtub Walls 32 • Install a Garage Door Opener 33 • Build a Pine Bookcase 35 • Install a Corner Cabinet 36 • Lay a Seamless Floor 38 • Replace a Kitchen Countertop 39 • Hang a Plank Ceiling 41 • Install a Closet Shelf System 42 • Replace a Double-Hung Window 44 • Add a Fireplace 45 • Secure a Front Door with a Deadbolt Lock 46 • Replace a Bi-Fold Closet Door 48 • Replace an Entrance Door 49 • Install Kitchen Cabinets 51 • Build an Eight-Foot Tile Countertop 52 • Lay Parquet Flooring 54 • Replace an Interior Door 55 • Lay Oak Strip Flooring 57 • Install a Fiberglass Tub Surround 58 • Install an Ironing Board Cupboard 60 • Rebuild a Window 61 • Install and Finish Recycled Wallboard 62

Chapter 3

Replace a Kitchen Sink and Faucet 64 • Install a Dishwasher 66 • Replace a Gas Water Heater 67 • Replace a Garbage Disposal 69 • Replace an Electric Water Heater 70 • Replace a Toilet 72 • Replace a Vanity and Faucet 73 • Replace a Kitchen Faucet 75 • Install a Water Softener 76 • Replace a Bathroom Faucet 78 • Install a Pedestal Sink 79 • Install a Hot Water Dispenser 80

Chapter 4

Install Track Lighting 82 • Install a Ductless Stove Hood Vent 84 • Install a Bathroom Vent/Light 85 • Replace a Kitchen Light 86 • Install a Ceiling Fan 87 • Install a Light Post 89 • Install a Porch Lantern 90 • Install a Circuit Panel Surge Protector 91 • Wire a Phone Extension 92

Chapter 5

Install an Attic Fan 94 • Caulk Windows 95 • Replace a Door Threshold 96 • Upgrade Attic Insulation With Fiberglass Batts 97 • Install a Furnace Humidifier 99 • Install an Electric Wall Heater 100 • Install a Central Vacuum System 101 • Add Six Inches of Loose-Fill Cellulose Insulation 103

Chapter 6

Replace a Sump Pump 105 • Clean a Chimney 107 • Secure a Sagging Ceiling 108 • Repair Window Glass 110 • Cure Brick Efflorescence 111 • Paint a Stained Ceiling 113 • Remove Textured Paint 114

Chapter 7

Install a Storm Door 116 • Install an Aluminum Storm Window 118 • Install a TV Antenna 119 • Install a Canvas Window Awning 120 • Install a New Garage Roof 122 • Replacing Vinyl Gutters and Downspouts 123 • Install a Mailbox on a Post 125 • Seal an Asphalt Driveway 126 • Paint a House 128 • Install a Weathervane 129 • Build a Redwood Deck 130 • Replace a Garage Door 132 • Power Wash a Deck 133 • Replace a Basement Door 134

Chapter 8

Install a Sprinkler System 136 • Lay a Brick Patio 138 • Laying Sod 139 • Build a Dog Kennel 140 • Build a 120-Foot Picket Fence with Gate 141 • Install a Flagpole 143 • Edge a Garden Bed 144 • Install a Stone Garden Path 145 • Build a Kid's Gym Set 146

Sources 148

DO IT YOURSELF ...OR NOT?

INTRODUCTION

We've been working on houses and writing about our home improvements for almost thirty years. We've done just about every job imaginable remodeling and repairing houses—we even moved a house from one location to another. When we began, we assumed we'd do all the work ourselves so we'd save a ton of money and get the job done right.

After the dust settled on our fourth house and we faced another house full of old hardwood floors that needed refinishing, we said, "Let's call a floor sander and see how much it costs to have it done." Even though we had refinished thousands of square feet of flooring, we weren't satisfied with the results and we were spending a small fortune renting the equipment.

When we got a reasonable bid from Hank, the floor sander, we divided the job so that he sanded and we applied the finish. The floors looked beautiful, and even with paying him, we were within our original budget and a week ahead of schedule.

Since then we've learned you don't have to do everything yourself—you can save time and money doing it yourself *and* hiring contractors.

We've analyzed one hundred of the most popular projects, to help you decide how to balance the two elements that always seem to be in short supply: your time and your money. This book will help answer the question: How much of the work can you—should you—do yourself?

For each project, you'll find an overview of what's involved and inside information we've learned: how much it costs, how much time is needed, what kind of talents and tools are required—all this—plus how much a contractor will charge to do the job.

We use cost data and time (in hours) data from contractors and for the DIY data our own hands-on experience. The figures are national averages, so they may be slightly higher or lower depending on your location. But the ratio (percent savings) between the professional job cost and the do-it-yourself savings will stay the same, no matter where you live.

1

This book is not a guide for estimating construction costs, but it gives you a realistic ballpark figure you can expect to spend on a project, and how much you can expect to save if you do it yourself.

Working on fourteen houses has taught us important lessons about home improvement projects, things that you should know before you tackle your next job:

- It takes much longer and often more money than planned.
- Even when there's a sizable savings by doing it yourself, the DIY Damage Factor makes it *not* a good idea.
- There are certain qualifiers to consider that sway the decision one way or the other.
- Factor in transporting materials and equipment.
- Renting special tools helps get the job done.
- Remember the value of your grunt work.

We recommend that some projects be left to a contractor and suggest that others are definitely do-able, even if you're not so handy. We include a Source List of specialty products and materials that you might find useful.

Before you tackle a project or call a contractor, look up the project here and see what our analysis and experience suggest. We just might surprise you.

CHAPTER
1

REMOVE WALLPAPER

Removing wallpaper is tedious, time-consuming and messy, but it saves you 90 percent of what a contractor charges. It's an ideal project for the first-time do-it-yourselfer because few skills are required, so a not-so-handy homeowner can tackle the job and be successful. A painting contractor charges $260 to remove wallpaper in a typical 10-by-12-foot room. You can do it yourself for about $25, which covers the cost of a putty knife, razor knife scraper, masking tape, plastic drop cloths and a quart of wallpaper remover. You will also need a bucket with a sponge mop or paint roller.

Removing wallpaper is easy if it's a single layer of old-fashioned paper wallpaper; it's more difficult if there are several layers or if it's been painted. Some washable wallcoverings made today are difficult to remove because they are water-resistant, and paint covering wallpaper makes it waterproof, so the water can't get behind the paper and soften the glue. If this is the case with your job, allow more time.

Mix the wallpaper remover and water according to the manufacturer's suggestions and make some slits in the paper so the solvent can soak in. Then use a sponge mop or paint roller dipped in the solvent and

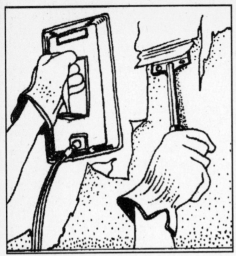

spread it on the wallcovering. Let the solvent soak into the paper for at least 20 minutes. Wet down two walls, then go back to the first wet wall and use the razor scraper to remove the wallpaper. Work ahead and wet down the next wall so the solvent has time to soak through the wallcovering. The whole job from start to finish will take a long day's work because in addition to the time-consuming removal, you should allow time to move all the furniture away from the walls.

If you have several rooms with wallpaper to remove, you can rent a wallpaper steamer for about $15 a day. But if you have to spread the work out over a long period of time, consider investing $50 in a wallpaper steamer designed for homeowners, which you can use when your time permits.

TIP BOX

Make your own wallpaper solvent by putting a few capfuls of fabric softener into a bucket of warm water to help loosen the wallpaper paste.

Use 1-inch-wide masking tape to attach a plastic drop cloth to the top of the baseboard molding of the walls. The wet, messy paper and paste residue will fall onto the plastic. Then when you're finished, wrap the gooey mess up and throw it away.

TABLE

Pro Cost	DIY Cost	DIY Saving	% Saving	Pro Time	DIY Time
$260	$25	$235	90	7	10

Refinish a Hardwood Floor

You can't beat the beauty and durability of a hardwood floor in any room in the house. Even one that's worn and scratched can be rejuvenated with sanding and refinishing. A professional floor refinisher charges about $2.30 a square foot to sand, stain and seal a hardwood floor. For a 14-by-20-foot room, that comes to $650. You can do it yourself for $100, which covers a day's rental of a drum sander and edger, the sheets of production-grade sandpaper needed and a gallon of penetrating stain sealer. It's heavy-duty work that will take you a good two days.

Despite the hefty 84 percent savings when you do it yourself, floor sanding is a job best left to professionals because of the potential damage it may inflict on your floor. Operating a drum sander without gouging the floor takes practice, and if you make a major mistake, the damage to the floor will quickly negate your savings. Floor sanding equipment is heavy and difficult to transport. It rarely fits into a standard car trunk, and if your work is on the second floor, it's a two-man job to muscle the equipment up there. While the professional floor refinisher babies his equipment and adjusts it regularly, the machines at a rental center may be out of adjustment and not working properly.

Before you decide whether to refinish a floor yourself or hire a refinisher, weigh these considerations. If you have a floor in only one room to refinish, you're better off hiring a pro. If you have a house full of floors that need refinishing and one room where you can practice, then the savings might outweigh the risk.

If you want to save some money, but can't decide if you want to do it yourself, consider hiring a pro to do the heavy sanding, and then you apply the finish.

> **TIP BOX**
>
> You'll find a nasty fine layer of grit throughout the house after floor sanding. To help contain the dust, tape heavy plastic sheeting to the door frames to seal off the room and open windows. If possible, leave the house when the sanding begins, to avoid inhaling the dust particles.

TABLE

Pro Cost	DIY Cost	DIY Saving	% Saving	Pro Time	DIY Time
$650	$100	$550	84	12	17

INSTALL CARPETING

The addition of wall-to-wall carpeting gives any room an instant facelift because it makes the space look larger and ties it all together. It makes a room warm and easier to clean since one sweep of a vacuum is all that's needed. A professional installer will charge $500 to lay 20 square yards of medium-grade nylon carpeting and padding in a typical 12-by-14-foot room. By laying the carpeting yourself you can save about half the cost.

The quality of the carpeting determines whether you should install it yourself or not. If the carpeting costs less than $12 a square yard, it's a good do-it-yourself project because if you damage the carpeting or make a wrong cut, you can recover from the mistake by buying more. If you totally botch the job, it will cost you money, but not a fortune.

The cost of installation is about the same regardless of the price of the carpeting. If you're using expensive material and ruin the installation, your recovery costs are substantially higher because you have to replace the carpeting—so you have more of your money at risk when installing expensive carpet.

Plan on spending at least $220 for carpeting and padding and about $30 to rent a carpet stretcher, kicker and seaming iron at a rental center or carpet store. Get instructions about operating them.

You should be able to complete the job in less than a day. If the room has old carpeting in it, by all means remove it yourself. That's the kind of grunt work you can't afford not to do, because no skills are needed, just your time.

TIP BOX

Before installing carpeting, remove the small quarter round molding along the baseboard. It's not necessary and you'll have a neater installation without it. Also vacuum the entire floor and use a crevice tool to remove dust and dirt from the joint between the floor and the baseboard.

TABLE

Pro Cost	DIY Cost	DIY Saving	% Saving	Pro Time	DIY Time
$500	$250	$250	50	4	7

ADD POLYSTYRENE MOLDING TO TRIM OUT A ROOM

You don't have to be a finish carpenter to trim out the doors and windows of a room, because new polystyrene molding systems make it a do-able project for a handy homeowner. Even flat, featureless walls can become the focal point of the room using this lightweight material that is easy to cut and install. Paint the new molding in a complimentary color and the room takes on an entirely new look.

Components of the systems are designed so that precision miter-joint cuts are not required. For example, one system uses inside and outside corner blocks that butt to straight-cut casings so you don't have to make miter cuts. Another system features all-in-one inside/outside premitered corner pieces and casings with predrilled holes that you align with dowels to assure a precise fit.

By doing it yourself, you'll pocket a 48 percent savings compared with hiring a carpenter. You should be able to complete the job in a couple of days. You'll need a handsaw, finishing nails, construction adhesive, latex caulk to fill any small gaps at the joints and paint.

To prepare the room for new trim, move the furniture to the center of the room. Then take down any window treatments so they're not in the way. Use a pry bar to remove any existing woodwork and trim at the doors, windows and floor. With a vacuum's crevice tool clean the areas around the windows and doors and along the baseboard, so they're free of dust and dirt.

You'll find these molding systems sold in home centers and at lumberyards.

TIP BOX

If you plan to paint the molding a contrasting color from the walls, paint the components before they're installed. Cut them to size and test fit them. Then number and label the back of each piece and paint with latex paint. When they're dry, install the components and caulk any openings. Touch up with paint the areas where caulk is visible.

TABLE

Pro Cost	DIY Cost	DIY Saving	% Saving	Pro Time	DIY Time
$625	$325	$300	48	12	18

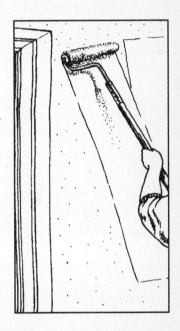

PAINT A ROOM

Painting is the most popular do-it-yourself project for a lot of reasons. It doesn't require expensive tools and equipment, you can learn how to paint on-the-job and it's very cost-effective when compared to hiring a contractor. You can paint the walls and ceiling in a typical 10-by-12-foot room for half of what a painting contractor charges. You can complete the job from start to finish in a day's time. For about $45 you can buy what you need: joint compound, two gallons of latex paint, a four-inch brush, roller pan, handle and sleeve (also called a roller cover) and plastic drop cloths.

The key to a professional-looking paint job is preparing the room and the surfaces, which usually requires more time than actually painting. Move all the furniture to the center of the room and cover it with old sheets or blankets. Roll up rugs and remove them, and cover wall-to-wall carpeting with plastic drop cloths taped with masking tape around the edges of the room. Remove wall hangings and pictures from the walls, and switch plate and electrical receptacle covers.

Remove dust and cobwebs from the walls and ceilings and wash off any dirt or grease marks. Patch any cracks and holes with a joint compound and sand them smooth before painting. If the walls or ceiling are badly cracked and need repair work, this will take more time.

TIP BOX

Troublesome stains from a marking or ballpoint pen will continue to bleed through new paint unless the stain is blocked. Use a fast-drying stain killer or spray shellac, which holds back the stain.

To clean out brushes and rollers, the pros use a paint spinner which spins out excess paint (like a kid's toy top) so the brushes and rollers don't harden as they dry. If you have several paint jobs planned, the paint spinner is a $20 investment you won't regret.

TABLE

Pro Cost	DIY Cost	DIY Saving	% Saving	Pro Time	DIY Time
$90	$45	$45	50	4	7

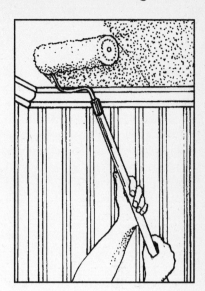

TEXTURE A CEILING

The Southwest look in decorating that's so popular today can be enhanced with a textured surface like a stucco ceiling. Since a ceiling often develops hairline cracks over the years, a heavy-bodied textured paint can be an ideal cover-up, as well. Textured paint can't hide the structural problems often found in an old plaster ceiling or camouflage a bad joint taping job on drywall, but it does a good job of covering up a less than perfect ceiling.

The paint is sold premixed in a two-gallon container, and it's ready to roll on, giving one-coat coverage for approximately 120 to 150 square feet of ceiling. For a typical 15-by-20-foot room ceiling the paint and textured paint roller handle and sleeve will cost about $40. Compare that with the $185 a painting contractor charges, and you'll see there's a handsome reward for doing it yourself.

You'll need a ladder, paint roller handle, sleeve and pan, scraper, sandpaper and electric sander, and some drop cloths.

You can complete the job in a day's time. Preparing the ceiling will take as much time as rolling on the textured paint, but it's an important first step. Protect the furnishings in the room by covering them with drop cloths, and remove and lower the cover plate on any ceiling lighting fixture so you have complete access to the ceiling. Protect a chandelier or light fixture by covering it with a large plastic garbage bag taped closed at the top.

If the ceiling isn't smooth, use a drywall compound to make it free of uneven surfaces so the new textured paint will be applied to a clean, level ceiling. When necessary, scrape away peeling paint and sand away any high spots. If you come across any stained areas, use a stain killer or spray shellac primer to hold back the stain.

To build the depth of texture that you want, work in sections of three feet square, applying a thin coat followed by a heavy cover over the wet thin coat. The texture paint roller sleeve has a looped nap that creates a tight stippled effect and rolls on the paint quite easily. For other finishing effects you can use a trowel, wide sponge or heavy bristle brush.

TIP BOX

Experiment with the roller to find the various textures you can create by applying degrees of pressure. Light pressure produces a stippled effect; heavy pressure creates a finer textured effect.

TABLE

Pro Cost	DIY Cost	DIY Saving	% Saving	Pro Time	DIY Time
$185	$40	$145	78	6	8

INSTALL
INTERIOR WINDOW SHUTTERS

Wooden shutters have been a classic window treatment for years because they are both versatile and practical. Shutters are ideal for a variety of decorating styles and their adjustable louvers let you control the amount of light and sun filtering into a room. You'll find them sold in many different widths and heights, either unfinished or painted. A carpenter charges about $130 to install unfinished pine shutters in a window that is 48 inches high by 48 inches wide. With some basic carpentry experience and tools you can install the shutters yourself for $70, which includes two pairs of two-panel unfinished pine (a total of eight shutters) and the hardware.

Even though there's a 46 percent savings by doing it yourself, it's worth hiring a carpenter if the window is badly out of square, because a carpenter has the expertise to custom cut the shutters to fit the not-so-perfect window jamb.

To see if a window is square, do this easy test: Measure the distance between opposite corners in two different directions and then compare the measurements. If they are exact or very close, your window is square, but if they differ by more than a half-inch, they're not square.

One way to install shutters is to first install one-by-two wood furring strips on the sides of the window jamb and shim the strips until they are parallel. Then install the shutters directly to the strips using hinged shutter hardware. You need basic carpentry tools, such as a saw, hammer, level, an electric drill, a screwdriver and measuring tape.

The job will take about four hours, but plan to spend additional time to stain or paint the shutters.

TIP BOX

Shutters look built into a window if they are finished the same color as the window trim, so before installing, paint or stain them on sawhorses where they can be turned over to finish both sides.

TABLE

Pro Cost	DIY Cost	DIY Saving	% Saving	Pro Time	DIY Time
$130	$70	$60	46	2	4

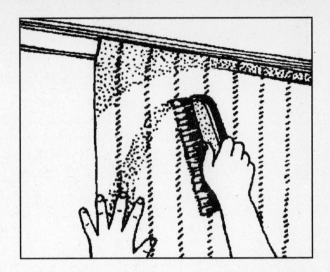

WALLPAPER A ROOM

The toughest part of hanging wallpaper has nothing to do with making the cuts and aligning the seams—it's choosing a pattern from the countless number of wallpaper books. By hanging wallpaper yourself, you can save more than half of what a professional paper hanger charges. For example, to wallpaper a typical 10-by-12-foot room with 350 square feet of wall area with an average price wallpaper ($15 a roll), it will cost about $425 for a professional job. You can do it yourself for $170, which includes the material, sizing for the wall and a wallpapering starter kit with a razor knife, plastic water tray, smoothing brush and seam roller. You'll also need a pair of scissors, tape measure, plumb line or carpenter's level, and an edging tool.

Despite the savings, don't do it yourself if you've chosen expensive wallcovering, because if you make some wrong cuts, you risk loosing a substantial investment. Consider hiring a pro if you're papering a two-story hallway that requires scaffolding, because it's expensive to rent.

If you're a first-time paper hanger, choose a room where you can practice the basic techniques. Don't attempt a room with sloped ceilings, dormers or tricky corners. A back bedroom is a good test bed; save the bathroom, kitchen and hallway for later. Plan on spending the better part of a day to complete the job from start to finish.

TIP BOX

For safety's sake: Turn off the electricity in the room so you don't hit a live wire when cutting paper around a receptacle or switch.

Wallcoverings that are vinyl-coated, fabric-backed and prepasted are the easiest to hang.

Patterns with a short repeat, such as a small check waste less paper aligning the designs. For example a paper with an 18-inch repeat must be moved at least 18 inches up or down to match the pattern.

TABLE

Pro Cost	DIY Cost	DIY Saving	% Saving	Pro Time	DIY Time
$425	$170	$255	60.0	4	9

INSTALL
VERTICAL BLINDS ON A PATIO DOOR

A patio door is an attractive feature because it opens a room with sunlight and creates a nice view of the outdoors. The downside, however, is that sunlight can be too strong, causing annoying glare and damaging furnishings. Fabric vertical blinds are a likely solution because you can adjust the amount of sunlight by turning the vanes and opening or closing them.

You'll spend about $160 for either light filtering or room darkening fabric-backed blinds to cover a typical 6-foot-wide-by-7-foot-high patio door. To have them installed runs about $80 more. You can do it yourself and save that expense, because it's easy to do and you probably already have the tools needed: a drill and bits, screwdriver and utility knife. It will take only a few hours and you'll enjoy the blinds for years to come.

When measuring for a vertical blind, note that the head rail must overlap (be wider then) the door opening at least three inches on each side for proper stacking of the vanes when the blinds are open. Depending on the length of the blind, you can mount it on the wall or the casing around the door frame. Mounting the blind on the wall gives you a little more flexibility in placement but be sure to secure the brackets to the wall studs with screws, or use large plastic wall anchors or Molly bolts. If you prefer to install the blind on the door casing, use the screws provided in the package.

Most units come with a valance that installs over the track for a nice finished look. Depending on the width of the door, the valance may have to be trimmed. First use a sharp utility knife to cut through the face of the valance to assure a clean cut.

TIP BOX

Before installing new vertical blinds, clean the sliding tracks of the patio door and free the weep holes of dirt so rainwater can flow out. If the inside door casing looks a bit dingy, give it a fresh coat of paint before the installation.

TABLE

Pro Cost	DIY Cost	DIY Saving	% Saving	Pro Time	DIY Time
$240	$160	$80	33	1	3

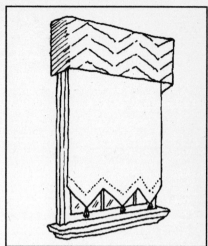

BUILD AND UPHOLSTER A WINDOW CORNICE BOARD

A cornice board is a window treatment used with a variety of different styles because, depending on the fabric used, it adapts to just about any home decorating scheme. It goes contemporary with a mini-blind or pleated shade and becomes more formal with tapestry drapes or sheers.

If you buy a custom-made cornice board from a window covering specialist or an interior designer, you'll pay about $35 a foot to have it built, plus the cost of the fabric. For example, a 40-inch-wide cornice will cost about $115 to build plus an additional $25 for the fabric.

You can make your own with a kit consisting of a one-inch-thick polystyrene board that is very easy to cut and glue together. The unit is made up of a front, top and two side boards. Once it is assembled, you pad the unit by gluing polyester batting (used for quilting) to its sides and front. You don't have to sew anything because the fabric is held in place with pins. All you do is drape the fabric over the padding, pull it tight and wrinkle-free and then secure it to the polystyrene with pushpins.

The panels are lightweight and held to the wall with self-stick adhesive back-mounting brackets. Your total investment is $55, which includes $25 for the kit, $10 for padding and $20 for fabric, and your investment in time is only a few hours.

TIP BOX

The easiest fabric to work with for a cornice board is a solid color or a random design or one that is wider than the cornice board, so you can use it running off the bolt, instead of having to seam two pieces of fabric together. If you choose a fabric with a vertical pattern such as a stripe, you may have to sew two pieces together so the stripes run vertically, not horizontally.

TABLE

Pro Cost	DIY Cost	DIY Saving	% Saving	Pro Time	DIY Time
$140	$55	$85	60	3	4

INSTALL PANELING

Wood paneling is one way to add warmth and interest to an otherwise featureless room. The natural look of wood in a home office or family room is especially appealing. Installing four-by-eight wood panels and trimming out the room is a job for any experienced do-it-yourselfer who has basic carpentry skills and tools.

To panel the walls of a 12-by-20-foot room and install new molding for trim costs $875 for 16 sheets of good quality ¼-inch-thick hardwood paneling, matching trim, adhesive and miscellaneous materials. A carpenter will charge $1,375 to do the job, so you'll save substantially by doing it yourself.

You can cut the panels by hand but there is a lot of ripping to do, so you really need a table saw. In addition you will need these basic carpentry tools: measuring tape, utility knife, hammer, nail set, level, block plane and a set of horses. Move all the furnishings to the center of the room so you'll be able to move the panels and position them. Set up a workstation in the room where you can stack the panels and set up a saw to cut them.

If the walls are sound, you can glue the paneling directly to them. But for badly crackled walls you should first install one-by-two wood furring strips to plumb up and level them.

Consider hiring a pro to install the paneling if the room has several doors and windows, because cutting and custom-fitting the paneling around existing woodwork calls for skills few do-it-yourselfers have.

You may find it's easier to remove all ceiling and floor moldings and window and door casing, rather than cut and fit the paneling around each opening. If this is the case, budget more time to carefully remove the trim and nails and reinstall it after the paneling is in place.

TIP BOX

If you're planning to panel a basement, check to see that there's not a high moisture level which would damage the paneling. Tape a 12-inch square of aluminum foil to an outside wall for a week. Check the foil and if there's beads of moisture on the side of the foil taped against the wall you have a problem. Cure this situation before installing the paneling.

TABLE

Pro Cost	DIY Cost	DIY Saving	% Saving	Pro Time	DIY Time
$1375	$875	$500	63	4	7

WAINSCOT A ROOM

Wainscoting is wooden paneling installed on the lower third of a wall and capped with chair rail molding. It originated in homes as a way of protecting the walls in dining areas and libraries from the scrapes and nicks of chairs as they were pushed away from a table or desk. Wainscoting is a popular addition to a room because it adds the warmth and richness of wood. The walls above can be decorated in a variety of ways, such as painting or wallcovering.

You can expect to pay a carpenter $385 to install 55 linear feet of wainscoting. If you have some carpentry experience and basic tools, you can tackle this job. Budget at least $165 to purchase unfinished pine, tongue and groove, beaded planking; adhesive and molding.

The most difficult part of this project is installing the wainscoting so it looks as if it matches the existing trim. Take a look at the door and window casings. If they are at least three-quarter-inch thick along the outside edge, there is a good chance you can butt the wainscoting up to the molding and it will look fine. If you have thinner door and window casing, call in a carpenter because the old moldings should be removed and then reinstalled over the wainscoting.

Allow yourself plenty of time to plan the job. Cutting the planks to length will go a lot faster if you use a circular saw, but it can be done with a handsaw. You'll need additional time to apply the finish and install the chair rail and molding to trim out the job.

TIP BOX

Wainscoting traditionally covers about 36 inches of the lower part of the wall.

You can save a lot of time finishing the wainscoting if you apply the first coat of finish before installing the planks. Apply finish to both sides of the planks to help control shrinkage during seasonal changes.

TABLE

Pro Cost	DIY Cost	DIY Saving	% Saving	Pro Time	DIY Time
$385	$165	$220	57	7	12

PAINT A WOODEN FLOOR

In the bedrooms of many older homes you'll find painted wood floors that have weathered many years. A coat of paint is an inexpensive facelift that even the most unhandy homeowner can successfully accomplish. The most tedious part of the job is emptying the room of furniture; the paint goes on easily and quickly.

You can do the job yourself in a few hours for $35, which includes a gallon of alkyd deck and floor enamel and two disposable roller covers.

You'll need to have on hand a paintbrush, roller pan, sleeve and handle with an extension pole, mineral spirits and steel wool.

A painting contractor will charge about $70, so you're saving 50 percent by doing it yourself.

Vacuum the floor to remove all the dust and dirt. Then use a hammer to drive in any loose nail heads so they're flush with the flooring. Remove all wax with a wax remover and scrub the floor with a steel wool pad dampened with mineral spirits to loosen the surface grime. If you have a large room, rent a floor buffer with steel wool pads for about $10 a day.

To apply the paint, use a brush to outline the edge of the room first, then use the roller to paint the floor. Begin painting the floor where the walls form the farthest corner of the room. Then work your way out of the room by painting from the far side to the door. Don't paint yourself into the room.

TIP BOX

If you don't have anywhere to store the furnishings, divide the job in half and prepare and paint one-half of the room while the other holds the furnishings.

Open the windows in the room so there's plenty of ventilation.

TABLE

Pro Cost	DIY Cost	DIY Saving	% Saving	Pro Time	DIY Time
$70	$35	$35	50	2	4

CHAPTER
2

INSTALL
QUARRY TILE IN A MUDROOM

Quarry tile is a good choice for the heavy traffic of a mudroom or back door entry because it is durable and easily maintained with the swipe of a wet mop. A tile installer will charge $370 to lay quarry tile using the "thin set" method in a 5-by-8-foot room. You can do it yourself and save 43 percent if you're a seasoned do-it-yourselfer with some tiling experience.

The materials needed will run you $210 for quarter-inch plywood underlayment, 40 square feet of 8-inch quarry tile, organic mastic and grout. Ask about borrowing a tile cutter, nipper and grout float, which are usually on loan where tiles are sold. Before you leave the store, try out the tools to make sure the cutter has sharpened blades (wheels). To rent the equipment costs about $15 a day. You'll also need a notched trowel and chalk line for layout.

Preparing the surface is an important step. It must be completely clean, smooth, dry, level and structurally sound. Lay down an underlayment or subfloor and secure it with glue and nails because a firm

foundation is the most significant factor to assure good results. Remove all the baseboard molding with a pry bar and hammer. If you plan to reuse the molding on top of the new tiles, be careful removing it; otherwise buy new molding to hide the rough edges of tiles against the wall.

Mark the center point of each wall in the room and snap two perpendicular chalk lines to find the center of the room. Then use these 90-degree markings as a guide as you work out from the center of the room. Lay tiles in one quadrant of the floor at a time.

Even though it's a relatively small space in which to lay tiles, there are many processes that make this a good day's worth of work.

TIP BOX

To help lay out tiles pick up a pack of inexpensive tile spacers. These cross-shaped pieces of plastic hold the tiles in alignment until the mastic sets up.

A pair of knee pads will save your knees and shins some wear and tear.

TABLE

Pro Cost	DIY Cost	DIY Saving	% Saving	Pro Time	DIY Time
$370	$210	$160	43	6	8

INSTALL A PET DOOR

We humans take the doors in a house for granted because we can open and close them, but from the family pet's perspective, doors can be very limiting. You can customize a house for your favorite dog or cat with a pet door so your pet can paw out to the porch or garage, or wherever his or her fancy goes. If you are handy with basic carpentry tools, you can install it yourself for the cost of the door, about $46. The wag of your pet's tail is payoff enough, but by installing the door yourself, you'll save 32 percent of the $70 a carpenter will charge.

The most intimidating part of the job is cutting a hole in your door, but it's easy to lay out the opening using the paper template provided. Use masking tape to secure the template where you plan to install the door and follow the guidelines which show exactly where to drill holes in the four corners of the unit. Cut right through the paper into the door so the new opening will be properly aligned. To install the pet door takes a few hours, and you need a saw, drill and screwdriver; screws are provided.

Read the directions from the manufacturer for any specific details and then determine the best location. A pet door looks best when it is centered in the lower half of the door, approximately three inches off the floor, or so your pet can easily step into the opening.

Pet doors are sold at pet stores and home centers and are available in sizes to fit small, medium and large animals. The door opening for the small doors is approximately 5 by 7 inches, for the medium 8 by 12 inches, for the large 11 by 16 inches and for the extra large 14 by 20 inches. The door has a push-flap and a removable, lockable panel that keeps unwanted visitors from entering.

If you have a metal exterior door, hire a carpenter to do the job.

TIP BOX

To prevent an unwanted pet from entering from the outside, pet doors come with a security panel. Hang the removable door panel on a hook near the pet door, where it's accessible and handy to use.

TABLE

Pro Cost	DIY Cost	DIY Saving	% Saving	Pro Time	DIY Time
$70	$46	$24	34	1	3

INSTALL PREFINISHED PLANK WOOD FLOORING

The addition of wood flooring can have a dramatic effect in a dining room or bedroom because it adds warmth and richness to an otherwise ordinary room. Prefinished plank flooring eliminates the finishing process because it comes stained and sealed, ready for installation. Despite that step-saving feature, its high cost limits it to being a project suitable for an experienced do-it-yourselfer only. If you don't have considerable carpentry skills, you're money ahead paying a professional installer.

You can expect to pay a professional about $1,600 to lay prefinished flooring in a typical 12-by-14-foot room. You can purchase the materials for $465, which includes the flooring and mastic, and install it yourself. Despite the potential 70 percent savings, jobs like this involving a hefty outlay for materials are best left to the pros.

If you decide to do it yourself, the job should take a long weekend of work. The tools needed to lay the floor include a circular saw, hammer mallet, chisel, chalk line and drill. You might consider renting a power nailer to make the job less difficult and time-consuming.

If the floor has several layers of old flooring to remove, that's where every do-it-yourselfer can get involved. You'll need a pry bar and pair of pliers to remove existing floor molding and nails. It's a strenuous job that's long on grunt work—that's why it's ideal for a do-it-yourselfer.

TIP BOX

Lay out the floor so the grain of the wood runs the length of the room.

Wear knee pads to prevent tiring your kneecaps.

TABLE

Pro Cost	DIY Cost	DIY Saving	% Saving	Pro Time	DIY Time
$1,600	$465	$1,135	70	10	21

INSTALL FOLD-AWAY ATTIC STAIRS

A fold-away stair unit taps a bounty of unused storage space in the attic with a convenient way to get to it. A typical unit is 25 inches wide, folds into three sections and fits a 9-foot-high ceiling.

A carpenter charges about $350 to install attic stairs, but if you have carpentry skills and tools, you can save more than half of that by doing the work yourself. Expect to spend $135 for a good-quality, clear pine fold-away stair assembly, plus $30 for additional framing lumber.

This is a job best left to a professional carpenter unless you have experience with house framing techniques, because the ceiling joists must be cut and reinforced with headers to prevent the ceiling from sagging. It's handy to have a helper in the attic to hold the unit in place while you work on a ladder in the room below. Expect to spend the better part of a day, maybe longer if you're working alone, to finish this project.

If you don't think you have the skill for the job, consider hiring a carpenter to install the stair unit, and after it is bolted into the rough opening in the ceiling, you can install the trim and paint the unit.

TIP BOX

When deciding the location for fold-away stairs consider the floor-plan in the room or hall where the unit will go. There should be room to walk around the stairs when they're unfolded and the unit shouldn't block a doorway or passage. Plan for maximum headroom at the top of the stairs in the attic so you can stand up. You don't want to reach the top stair and hit your head on the rafters.

TABLE

Pro Cost	DIY Cost	DIY Saving	% Saving	Pro Time	DIY Time
$350	$165	$185	52	3	10

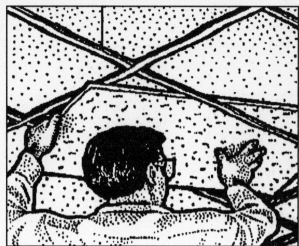

INSTALL A SUSPENDED CEILING

A suspended ceiling can give a room makeover the finishing touch that ties it all together, providing a continuous stretch of acoustical tiles mounted in a streamline metal track. It can also be a problem solver and conceal a bad ceiling, lower energy costs and deaden sound within the room. You can install the ceiling yourself for the cost of the materials, which is about $155 for a typical 10-by-12 foot room. A contractor will do the work for $275 so you save more than 40 percent by doing it yourself.

Ceiling systems are designed to be easy to install so you'll need only basic carpentry tools: hammer, pliers, metal snips, utility knife, carpenter's level, chalk line and measuring tape. You'll need to have a ladder, or two of them if you're working with a helper. The components of the grid include main runners, cross tees, wire fasteners, hanger wires and wall molding.

It will cost you more money and take longer if there are obstructions such as protruding overhead pipes or soffits that you have to work around and frame out. If you want to include fluorescent lighting fixtures that drop in place, hire an electrician to install them.

The job takes a long day's work and most of the time is spent planning and appraising the ceiling and laying out the grid system. You won't see the transformation until the grid is in place and you're ready to place the tiles into it.

TIP BOX

Most building requirements call for a minimum height of 7½ feet for a basement or attic ceiling; you'll need several more inches to allow for framing and the grid system.

When installing and cutting the tiles, wear safety glasses, gloves and long-sleeved clothing because the material contains mineral fiber or fiberglass which may cause temporary irritation.

TABLE

Pro Cost	DIY Cost	DIY Saving	% Saving	Pro Time	DIY Time
$275	$155	$120	43	10	13

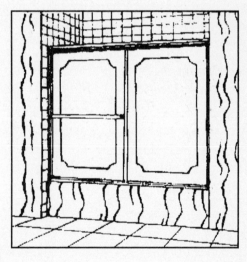

INSTALL A SLIDING TUB DOOR

A shower curtain adds a decorative touch to a bathroom, but its damp surface is a breeding ground for mildew and it's difficult to keep clean and dry. A sliding tub door, on the other hand, helps eliminate the mildew problem and creates a clean, contemporary look. Tub door enclosures are designed with either two or three movable panels made of decorative tempered safety glass, fiberglass or plastic. Some have a glass mirrored panel and include a towel bar so they do double duty— an important feature in a small bathroom where space is at a premium.

The enclosure has side tracks at the front and rear to support the door at the top and bottom. There are weep holes for drainage in the lower track, mounted on the tub.

These assemblies are designed for do-it-yourself installation, so they come packaged with explicit directions. A good-quality sliding door costs about $200. Many home centers offer an installed price of about $420, which gives you a good idea how much the labor is worth. By doing it yourself, you can save more than 50 percent.

The job will take about five hours, and before you begin, read the step-by-step directions and assemble these tools: an electric drill, carpenter's level, hacksaw and screwdriver. Lay out, measure and cut the tracks that support the doors, and then assemble the components together. If not included with the tub door, buy a tube of silicone bathtub caulk to seal gaps between the track and tub surround.

TIP BOX

You'll need a carbide-tipped masonry drill bit to make pilot holes in ceramic tile for the mounting screws or wall anchors. Check the instructions to see what size bit you will need.

TABLE

Pro Cost	DIY Cost	DIY Saving	% Saving	Pro Time	DIY Time
$420	$200	$220	52	2	5

INSTALL CERAMIC TILE ON BATHTUB WALLS

The three walls surrounding a bathtub are in continual contact with water and moisture which can damage them and provide an ideal breeding ground for mildew. Ceramic tile is one of the most durable materials for covering these walls and it can be successfully installed by an experienced do-it-yourselfer.

Assuming the walls around the tub are sound, a tile installer will charge $410 to do the job. But you can buy the tiles, mastic and grout for $125 and do it yourself, saving almost 70 percent. The job will take two full days to plan the layout and install and grout the tiles. Double the figure if you choose custom tile.

You need a carpenter's level, chalk line, notched trowel, tile cutter and nipper, grout float and a bucket for mixing the grout. Often you can borrow or rent these tools from the tile supplier where you purchase the tile. If you are considering doing more than one tiling project, you can buy inexpensive tiling tools at tile and home centers.

If the walls are rotten or damaged, replace them before installing the tile. For the best results use cement board, a water- and rot-resistant wallboard material. It's more expensive than wallboard, but it's the best choice for a tile backer. To cut costs use cement board on the lower third of the wall, around the tub area, where the wall is most vulnerable to moisture damage, with wallboard above it.

TIP BOX

It's difficult to trim cut tile by less than one inch, so plan the layout of the tiles to avoid these sliver-like cuts.

Your shoes can damage the surface of the bathtub while you stand in it, so protect the tub bottom with pieces of heavy cardboard, drop cloths or old blankets.

TABLE

Pro Cost	DIY Cost	DIY Saving	% Saving	Pro Time	DIY Time
$410	$125	$285	70	10	17

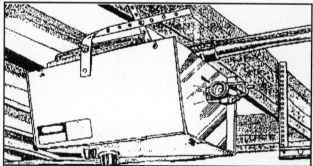

INSTALL A GARAGE DOOR OPENER

If you've never had a garage door opener, you don't know what you're missing. For many of us it's a convenience in the same league as a washing machine because it gets you out of the car and into your house quickly and safely, especially during inclement weather. You can buy and install an electric door opener with a remote unit for $180 or pay an installer $356 to have it done professionally. By doing it yourself, you save almost 50 percent, so it's a job worth considering even if you're a first-time do-it-yourselfer.

By law all garage-door openers sold in the United States must be equipped with an entrapment-protection device, which prevents the door from closing when an object blocks the path of the infrared beam. So when you're shopping for an opener, choose one designed so it won't close every time it senses something in its path.

Most garage door openers are designed for easy installation and come with complete instructions. To install it yourself, you'll need a sturdy ladder and these tools: hammer, screwdriver, adjustable wrench (a socket wrench is very handy), pliers, carpenter's level and measuring tape. It will take you a good six hours to assemble the opener, attach it to the door, hang the power unit from the ceiling and connect it to an electrical source. Enlist someone to help you which will save you many trips up and down the ladder.

TIP BOX

Check that your garage door is properly balanced by raising it about three feet off the ground. If it continues to move up or down on its own, call a garage door service to adjust the amount of tension on the door spring.

TABLE

Pro Cost	DIY Cost	DIY Saving	% Saving	Pro Time	DIY Time
$356	$180	$176	49	4	6

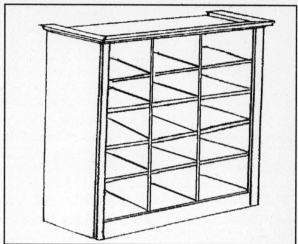

BUILD A PINE BOOKCASE

Anyone with an appreciation of handcrafted woodwork sees the value of a custom-built bookcase. It adds architectural detail and interest, while providing convenient storage space and display area for favorite things. To have a cabinetmaker build a classically designed three-bay bookcase that measures 54 inches wide will cost $700. If you have the woodworking skills, you can build it yourself for $250, saving you more than half of what a cabinetmaker charges.

As a first-time carpentry project a bookcase is going to take at least a weekend of work, and additional time to finish or paint the unit. The $250 will cover the materials you need: select-grade 1-by-12-inch pine, glue, fasteners and shelf hardware. Use 1-by-12 lumber so you can avoid ripping or cutting down the length of the boards and save time by not having to edge-glue narrow boards together.

You'll need basic carpentry tools, and a circular or table saw will make the job easier and the cuts more accurate. Remember: Measure twice and cut once, because if you make a wrong cut, you'll have to buy more material, which gets expensive.

Choose a work area where you have room to move around the unit as you cut the long parts and assemble and finish the bookcase. A garage or basement workshop with good ventilation is ideal.

Plan on spending more time if you want to build the bookcase into a wall, because you'll have to prepare the area by removing the base-board trim and probably have to make adjustments to custom fit the unit in place.

TIP BOX

If you are going to paint the bookcase, you can save money by substituting particle board for the back of the unit.

To avoid a blotchy finish, prime the cabinet before painting it and use a wood conditioner before staining.

TABLE

Pro Cost	DIY Cost	DIY Saving	% Saving	Pro Time	DIY Time
$700	$250	$450	64	12	25

INSTALL A CORNER CABINET

A corner cabinet in a dining room adds the look and appeal of traditional refinement while offering practical built-in storage for china and serving pieces. To custom build one requires the skills of a cabinetmaker, but you can buy one already made. Even a first-time woodworker can install a corner curio cabinet, because the carpentry work involved isn't very difficult.

For $260 you can buy an assembled, ready-to-finish pine corner cabinet and the materials to finish and install it. A carpenter will charge $430 for the job, so by doing it yourself you can save 40 percent.

You'll need only basic carpentry tools and a few pieces of scrap wood for shims.

Transporting the cabinet and maneuvering it into the house is the most challenging part of the job, because of its bulky size. If you have a van, station wagon or pickup truck, it's no problem. If you don't, pay the delivery charge to assure that the cabinet arrives without any nicks or bumps.

To install the cabinet remove the baseboard from the walls that the cabinet will lie against. Put the molding aside until after you have installed the cabinet, then trim the molding to fit and reinstall it. Stand the cabinet in place and work slowly, checking the fit as you progress. Rarely will walls be square or plumb, so expect to plane down or cut the cabinet sides to make it fit flush in the corner. It'll take about five hours to install.

Finishing the cabinet will probably take more time than installing it, because of the drying required between coats of finish. You can save some time and get better results if you apply the first coats of stain and finish before installing the cabinet.

Reinstall the floor molding, cutting it short to butt against the new corner unit.

TIP BOX

After the cabinet's finish is dry, fill all the nail holes with a colored wax crayon. These crayons are sold in a wide variety of shades at paint stores and home centers.

TABLE

Pro Cost	DIY Cost	DIY Saving	% Saving	Pro Time	DIY Time
$430	$260	$170	40	3	5

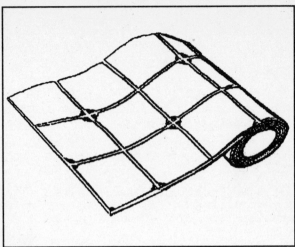

LAY A
SEAMLESS FLOOR

By replacing an old, worn floor with a new, resilient, seamless floor, you accomplish a lot more than a dramatic transformation. New flooring material is cushioned so that it's comfortable to stand on for long periods of time, is easy to clean and maintain and makes the room look larger.

Seamless flooring material ranges in price so the choice depends on your budget and your taste. If you've chosen a moderately priced material and have an uninterrupted floor, without cabinets or islands to cut around, laying a seamless floor is a do-able do-it-yourself project. However, if you're laying an expensive piece of flooring and the configuration of the room requires several precision cuts, consider hiring a professional installer. Only someone with experience should work with high-end materials, because if you have to replace the material because of a wrong cut, you've canceled any savings you might have earned.

To lay a moderately priced seamless floor in a 10-by-12-foot room, the material will cost $275, which includes the flooring, adhesive, seam sealer and metal finish strip for the doorway. An installer charges $490 for the same job, so you'll realize a 43 percent savings by doing it yourself.

Plan on spending a day to complete the job. You'll need to have on hand a utility knife, straightedge and a notched trowel for spreading the adhesive. Rent a floor roller for about $10 a day to seal the seams and adhesive.

Resilient flooring can be installed over another floorcovering if the existing flooring is a smooth, level surface without a deeply embossed pattern. If not, a subfloor of plywood called underlayment should be applied over the tile or existing flooring because without it, the outline of the tiles or pattern will show through. Plan on removing the base shoe molding, which is the half-round strip of wood that conceals the floor joint. Use a chisel and putty knife to work it free and away from floor molding.

If the existing floor needs extensive repair work to make it level, consider hiring a pro. If you want to do part of the job, tear out the old floor before underlayment and new flooring are laid.

TIP BOX

Move the flooring material into the room a few days before installation so it can "relax" and adjust to the temperature.

TABLE

Pro Cost	DIY Cost	DIY Saving	% Saving	Pro Time	DIY Time
$490	$275	$215	43	5	9

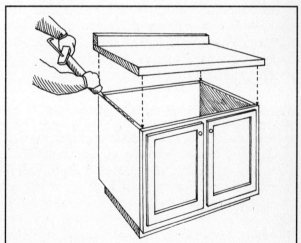

REPLACE A KITCHEN COUNTERTOP

The countertop is the hardest working surface in a kitchen because it's where most of the chores take place. It's also a dominant element in a kitchen design because it outlines the room and anchors the cabinets.

You can do this project yourself or hire a contractor, depending on your skills and the condition of your cabinets and walls. The job involves removing the old countertop first and then fastening the new countertop to the base cabinets. A new countertop 15 feet long, of good quality plastic laminate, with a rolled front edge and 4-inch backsplash, will cost $230. A contractor will charge $480 to remove the old countertop and install the new one.

If you have carpentry experience, you can tackle this job and pocket a sizable 52 percent savings, but if the countertop has several mitered corners or the walls are badly out of square, you're better off having them professionally replaced.

Bring along an accurate drawing of the kitchen, with precise measurements of the cabinets and walls, when ordering the material. To be on the safe side, have the job figured and checked by a professional if it's a large kitchen or has unusual angles or cuts. Don't forget to order matching end caps to finish off all exposed counter ends.

To find out how to remove the old countertop, you'll have to investigate to see how and where it's attached to the base cabinets. This might involve removing drawers and the contents of cabinets.

From removing the old countertop to completing the job should take a good ten hours, because precise workmanship takes time. Even if you don't plan to do the entire job yourself, you can do the grunt work of removing the old countertops.

TIP BOX

If your eyesight is failing, choose a countertop with a color that contrasts with your dishes and pans, which makes them easier to see.

TABLE

Pro Cost	DIY Cost	DIY Saving	% Saving	Pro Time	DIY Time
$480	$230	$250	52	7	10

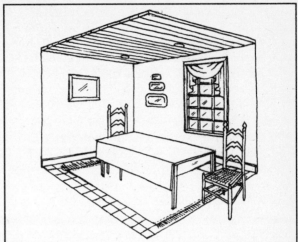

HANG A PLANK CEILING

The look of a natural wood ceiling goes hand in hand with both contemporary and country furnishings, which makes it a popular choice in decorating a home today. While it used to take the fine workmanship of a finish carpenter to custom fit wooden planks on a ceiling, it's much easier today, using a plank ceiling system designed for a do-it-yourselfer to install.

The system consists of ceiling tiles cut to resemble wooden planks. These tiles have a realistic wood-grain finish and are designed with tongue-and-groove edges that fit together with clips on either wood furring strips or metal tracks.

A carpenter will charge about $275 to install a plank ceiling in a 10-by-12-foot room. You can buy the materials for about $110, which also includes the cost of wooden molding to trim out the ceiling and cap the edges of the planks where they meet the walls. The tools needed to complete the job include a chalk line, measuring tape, hammer, staple gun with staples and handsaw. You'll also need a ladder. The job should take a good day's work, with much of your time spent planning, so the track is installed securely and level. Work slowly and check your work carefully. You'll pocket a 60 percent savings.

If your ceiling is a flat surface with no obstructions, it's a job any handyman can successfully accomplish. If there are pipes or heating ducts hanging below the ceiling, a soffit should be built to frame them out. Then the planks are installed on top of the soffit as if it were the ceiling. This kind of job is best left to a craftsman who has carpentry experience.

TIP BOX

If your ceiling is sagging, repair it before installing a ceiling system to cover it up. Use plaster washers to fasten the sagging areas to the framing or lath behind them.

TABLE

Pro Cost	DIY Cost	DIY Saving	% Saving	Pro Time	DIY Time
$275	$110	$165	60	4	7

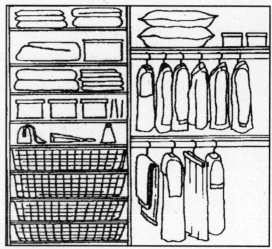

INSTALL A CLOSET SHELF SYSTEM

You can double the usable space in a closet by reorganizing it and using a shelving system with components to categorize the items. Installing a plastic-coated wire shelving system is easy and it's a job you'll enjoy every time you open the closet door. The real challenge is getting rid of all the stuff that's in the closet but seldom used. Go through the contents and discard what you don't use and pack it off to a charitable organization or take it to a resale shop.

It costs $115 to install a shelving system in a typical 6-foot-wide-by-24-inch-deep closet with the following components: three shelves, a tier of four short shelves supported by horizontal rails, a hanging organizer and four stacking baskets. A carpenter will charge about $185 for the system and installation, so there's a 36 percent savings by doing it yourself.

Emptying the closet, removing the existing rod and shelf and installing the new system takes about five hours. The steps you follow are these: lay out the job, install screw-in clips in the walls of the closet, install brackets that hold the shelves in place and assemble the components.

The only tools needed are a level, pencil, screwdriver and drill. There are several manufacturers of these systems and most of them offer very thorough planning guides and installation instructions. Take a shopping expedition to a home center or closet store to look at the systems available and see what components are included. For the system you like bring home a planning guide which explains how to measure your closet and plan a design.

TIP BOX

For a deluxe job, give the closet a quick coat of paint while it is empty and before you install the shelving system.

TABLE

Pro Cost	DIY Cost	DIY Saving	% Saving	Pro Time	DIY Time
$185	$115	$70	36	2	5

REPLACE A DOUBLE-HUNG WINDOW

Installing a replacement window isn't a trivial project, but it's certainly within the realm of someone with carpentry experience. A window contractor who does this every day has developed tricks to speed the job along, so a high percentage of the cost is for the window itself. For $235 you can have a 3-by-4-foot double-hung thermopane window (either vinyl or aluminum clad) installed, or you can buy the window for $160 and make the swap, pocketing a 32 percent savings. If you have an odd-sized window, it will cost more to custom build a replacement. You can use a smaller window and have the opening built up with extra framing so it fits, but that raises the cost of labor.

A window contractor who does this every day can retrofit a window with a new unit in less than four hours; it will take you much longer, especially if you're working on a ladder with a second-story window. It's useful to have a helper on hand to manhandle the unit and work with you shimming and adjusting it. You'll need basic carpentry tools, and a circular saw will speed things along if you have to cut any of the framing. Budget more time and money to replace and paint the exterior siding, make repairs to wallboard drywall and reinstall the interior woodwork.

> **TIP BOX**
>
> It is a lot easier to replace a window with one that is slightly smaller, rather than larger, because you can use wider trim to make up the difference in size. When installing a replacement window that's larger than the old one, you have to cut into the wall and framing members of the building.

TABLE

Pro Cost	DIY Cost	DIY Saving	% Saving	Pro Time	DIY Time
$235	$160	$75	32	4	10

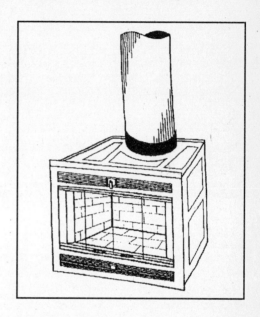

ADD A FIREPLACE

Most realtors will tell you that a fireplace is a good investment because it's a popular selling feature of a house. Some of the figures we've seen suggest there's close to 100 percent payback when you put the house on the market. This analysis is for installing a zero-clearance gas fireplace which can be installed with a direct vent through a wall, even when there's no room for a chimney.

An experienced do-it-yourselfer can do the job, but we'd suggest hiring a contractor because it's a hefty investment and there's no fudge factor. It's got to be done right the first time.

A contractor will charge $2,245 to install a prefab zero-clearance fireplace and chimney. You can purchase the basic components for about $1,650 and install it, saving 26 percent. Budget extra funds for framing lumber and wallboard needed to finish off the fireplace or enclose the chimney. Workwise, it will take at least a week to complete this project.

Before you begin planning or purchasing anything, check with your local building department. All building codes must be strictly followed. If the fireplace and its installation don't meet codes, you can't expect to recover any of your investment; in fact, you might not be able to sell your house until the corrections are made.

TABLE

Pro Cost	DIY Cost	DIY Saving	% Saving	Pro Time	DIY Time
$2,245	$1,650	$595	26	29	40

SECURE A
FRONT DOOR WITH A DEADBOLT LOCK

Standard security measures at home begin with a deadbolt lock on all entry doors because its design makes it a difficult lock to break. While the addition of a double cylinder deadbolt lock is added security on any door, it's especially important for a door with a glass pane which can be broken to gain access to the inside. A deadbolt is keyed on both sides of the door so that even if an intruder brakes the glass, a key will be needed to unlock the door from the inside as well as the outside.

You can install a deadbolt lock for about $55, which covers the cost of the lock, a door lock installation kit, a hole cutter for a drill and a spade bit to make small holes in the edge of the door. A locksmith charges $110, so you'll save half by doing it yourself. While installing a lock may sound intimidating, it's a do-able job for a first-time handyman because it requires more patience and precision workmanship than it does experience and tools.

The job uses a paper template which comes packaged with the lock and instructions as to where layout holes should be cut. You tape the template to the door and drill holes through it. When the holes are drilled, they're properly aligned for installing the lock. You'll use a screwdriver, try square, chisel and electric drill to install the new lock. All told it should take you about two hours.

TIP BOX

Before installing a new lock, decide if the door needs a new paint job, because it's easier to paint when the old lock is removed and before installing the new one.

TABLE

Pro Cost	DIY Cost	DIY Saving	% Saving	Pro Time	DIY Time
$110	$55	$55	50	1	2

REPLACE A BI-FOLD CLOSET DOOR

Wooden bi-fold door panels come in a variety of styles, which are flat, louvered or paneled. Some have glass inserts and are mirrored, so the choice is diverse and depends on your budget and style. Even a first-time do-it-yourselfer can make the replacement with a minimum of tools and time and save more than half of what a carpenter would charge.

Expect to pay a carpenter $250 to install the doors. For $110 you can buy four solid wood, raised paneled doors and hardware to fit an average 40-inch-wide closet door.

Measure the old door panels and buy new ones the same size so you're sure they will fit in the opening. When you remove the old panels, notice how they're installed on the hardware and attached to the doorjamb. The installation should take you a few hours and it's helpful to have someone available to hold the panels as you align them with the hardware. You'll need some basic tools like a hammer, an electric drill, a measuring tape and screwdriver to remove the old door and its hardware and rehang the new one.

You don't have to empty the closet to replace the doors, but you do need room to stand in it when installing the hardware. If you're using the existing hardware and the new screws are loose in the old screw holes of the doorjamb, try this trick: Dip wooden match sticks into white glue and force them into the holes to fill them. As the glue dries, drive the screw into the hole.

If you wish to paint or finish the door panels with stain, do it before you install them in the closet. Lay them down on a set of sawhorses so they are easy to work on. If you're staining them, use a wood conditioner on the wood first to prevent blotchy results.

TIP BOX

When bi-fold doors are open, they block part of the opening so it's difficult to reach into corners. To gain complete access, replace the existing hardware with "Full Access Folding Door Hardware," which has a special track and arm that swing open so the door panels can swing back and fold flat against the wall. This is especially useful when a laundry or desk area is tucked into a closet.

TABLE

Pro Cost	DIY Cost	DIY Saving	% Saving	Pro Time	DIY Time
$250	$110	$140	56	3	2

REPLACE AN ENTRANCE DOOR

A visitor's first impression of your house is often its front door so its quality and condition are of vital importance. Replacing a front door for one that's more attractive and secure has never been more do-able for a homeowner, because of prehung door units designed and engineered for easy installation. The replacement door is a metal-clad solid-core unit complete with jamb and weatherstripping and designed to fit into your existing doorjamb. A carpenter will charge $295 to install the door, or you can buy one for $210, do the work yourself and pocket a nice 28 percent savings.

Most replacement units are sized to fit standard doorjambs and they are sold at lumberyards and home centers. When shopping for one, bring a sketch of the door opening, with accurate measurements of the existing door. If the store doesn't carry the size you need, they can often special order a door to fit any opening.

Removing the existing door is the most arduous part of this project. The new door is prehung on a new jamb so installation is straightforward and will take a day's work. You can save time by painting the doorjamb and trim before you install them.

If your door is odd-sized or unusually small, you may not be able to use a stock door. If that's the case, the doorjamb needs to be modified, which is a job best left to a carpenter, unless you're skilled in carpentry.

TIP BOX

Bring a snapshot of the door you're replacing so you don't get confused as to which side the hinges should be on the new door.

TABLE

Pro Cost	DIY Cost	DIY Saving	% Saving	Pro Time	DIY Time
$295	$210	$85	28	2	7

INSTALL
KITCHEN CABINETS

If new cabinets are part of your kitchen remodeling plans, look at the walls to decide if you should hang the cabinets yourself. If the walls are straight, level and plumb and you're an experienced do-it-yourselfer, you can install the cabinets. But if it's an old house with out-of-square walls, consider hiring a carpenter who can easily make the necessary adjustments and custom fit the cabinets to the walls.

By doing it yourself, you'll save more than 30 percent of what a carpenter charges, which is $670 for ten feet of wall-mounted, two-door, medium-grade, prefinished wood cabinets. You can buy the cabinets for $450 and hang them using basic carpentry tools and a ladder. You'll need a van or truck to transport them or you'll have to pay extra to have them delivered.

Clear an area near the kitchen to store the cabinets, because they're large and bulky. As soon as they arrive unpack them to see that they're what you ordered and are not damaged. Measure them to make sure they'll fit and check that the hinges are on the correct side.

Usually cabinets are attached to the wall at the top and bottom mounting rails with wood screws driven into the studs behind the walls. When installing, make sure that the cabinet is level and plumb and use shims wedged behind and under wherever needed.

To connect wall-hung cabinets, first clamp them together, and when they are level and plumb, screw them together.

TIP BOX

Label the cabinets with masking tape or Post-it notes with things written on them like "above refrigerator," "left side of range," etc., so you know where to install them.

To hold a cabinet in place while adjusting it for installation, make a temporary cleat using a two-by-four furring strip of lumber. Put the strip where you want the bottom of the cabinet located and then rest the back edge of the cabinet on the strip while you fasten the cabinet at the top. Remove the strip after the cabinets are secure. The strip will leave a few small nail holes to fill in later.

TABLE

Pro Cost	DIY Cost	DIY Saving	% Saving	Pro Time	DIY Time
$670	$450	$220	32	2	4

BUILD AN EIGHT-FOOT TILE COUNTERTOP

A ceramic tile countertop can dramatically change the appearance of a kitchen or bathroom while providing a colorful and durable work surface that will last a long time. The hardworking material is best installed over a solid base of half-inch plywood and a cement backer board. A carpenter will charge $345 to build a custom eight-foot counter and you can do it yourself for about $120, saving 65 percent.

The materials needed to build an 8-foot-long, 25-inch-deep counter top are two 4-by-8 sheets of half-inch plywood and cement board, grout, grout sealer, mastic and 20 square feet of ceramic tile. For edging, choose tile that has matching bull nose trim, or special edging tiles called v-caps and outside corner caps. Ask to borrow or rent a tile cutter and water-cooled tile saw to help you with intricate cuts. Have on hand nippers, a notched trowel, hand trowel, rubber float, tape measure, chalk line and carpenter's level. It's a weekend's worth of work.

If you don't have any experience with carpentry, consider hiring a carpenter to build the base and then you can take your time and apply the tile.

You can apply tile to an existing countertop if the base of the countertop is secured to the base cabinets. Remove all traces of wax, oil and dirt before applying the tile.

TIP BOX

If there's an electrical outlet or receptacle near the area where you're working, turn off the electricity to it for shock protection and cover it with masking tape to protect it from adhesive or grout.

Use a clear silicone caulk on any joints where the tile meets another material.

TABLE

Pro Cost	DIY Cost	DIY Saving	% Saving	Pro Time	DIY Time
$345	$120	$225	65	8	11

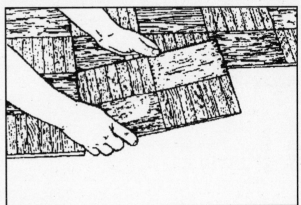

LAY
PARQUET FLOORING

The rich, intricate pattern of parquet floor tiles adds interest and appeal to any room. The 12-inch tiles are sold at flooring outlets and home centers prefinished in light and dark stains and run about $3 a piece. The tiles are best installed on a smooth subfloor in good structural condition. Remove multiple layers of flooring and make any repair work that's required before installing the new floor tiles.

For a 240-square-foot area of a hall or foyer the material cost is $900, which includes the parquet tiles, mastic and underlayment and trim. A flooring contractor will charge $1,550 for the job and it's money well spent if you have little carpentry experience. But if you are careful and don't rush the project, it's a job you can tackle and save 41 percent. Keep in mind that the high cost of the materials puts a considerable amount of your money at risk if you botch the job. Your potential savings can be quickly eaten up if you waste a lot of material.

To complete the two-day job you'll need basic carpentry tools and either a circular saw or fine-toothed handsaw for cutting the tiles. Each box of tiles comes with an instruction sheet. Read it carefully and follow the layout and installation suggestions. Few rooms in older houses are square, so you will have to cut a lot of tiles to form the border. Invest in a pair of knee pads and you won't have sore shins or aching knee joints.

Store the floor tiles in the room where they'll be laid, so they can adjust to the moisture and expand or contract.

TIP BOX

To prevent ragged edges when cutting the tiles, put them facedown if you're using a power circular saw, and faceup when cutting with a handsaw.

If the tiles have a paper backing, be careful to dispose of it because it's slippery and can cause someone to fall.

TABLE

Pro Cost	DIY Cost	DIY Saving	% Saving	Pro Time	DIY Time
$1,550	$900	$650	41	12	17

REPLACE AN INTERIOR DOOR

When a door in a hallway or room looks good, it goes unnoticed, but when it's banged up or damaged, it's an unpleasant eyesore. Because of its lightweight construction, an interior hollow-core door sometimes ends up with holes or becomes warped by moisture. If you replace a standard hollow-core door with a 5-panel solid pine door, you'll see a noticable improvement.

Hanging a door involves the most basic carpentry skills that most first-time do-it-yourselfers have. You can buy a paneled door at a home center or lumberyard for about $65, install it in half a day and save more than half of the $140 a carpenter will charge.

You probably already have the tools you need: a measuring tape, screwdriver, chisel, hammer and electric drill with a hole saw large enough to cut the hole for the lock set. If the new door is too long, you'll need a hand or circular saw to trim it at the bottom.

The job involves removing the old door and salvaging hinges and door lock if they're in good condition. Budget an additional $30 to $40 if you decide to replace the hinges and lock set. Marking the location and cutting the hinge mortises on the door calls for precision, so work slowly. For about $10 you can rent a nifty tool used by the professionals. It's a hinge-locating template that is used with a router that cuts the hinge mortises on both the door and jamb.

If you have no carpentry experience at all, do the grunt work of removing the old door and hardware and call in the carpenter to hang the new door.

TIP BOX

With the door out of the frame, it's the ideal time to paint the jambs or sides of the frame. Don't forget to paint all edges of the door, especially at the top or bottom if you cut it to prevent warping.

TABLE

Pro Cost	DIY Cost	DIY Saving	% Saving	Pro Time	DIY Time
$140	$65	$75	53	1	4

LAY OAK STRIP FLOORING

Natural wood floors have never been more popular than they are today and they're available in a variety of designs, from the traditional random strips to those with intricate inlays and patterns. Unless you're an experienced craftsman, this is a job best left to a flooring contractor because of the high cost of the materials. With a professional installation you can be assured of a lifetime improvement that will be a handsome and durable floor and an enhancement to the house.

To lay new unfinished oak strip flooring in a typical 15-by-20-foot room, a flooring contractor will charge $1,800. You can purchase the materials for $1,275 and do it yourself, saving 30 percent. But the DIY damage factor should be considered because if you miscut the material and have to replace it, you're money behind, not ahead.

An old floor that needs to be ripped up and removed is a good job for a handy homeowner who is long on time and low on talent. It's the epitome of grunt work because it requires little in the way of skills or tools; what's needed is a lot of man-hours to muscle the old flooring up and out of the room.

Another job to consider is making repairs that might be needed on the subfloor. These labor-intensive jobs can double the total job time, so you'll save money tackling them. The idea is to pay the contractor for expertise and skill in laying a floor, not to do menial work anyone, even you, can do.

TABLE

Pro Cost	DIY Cost	DIY Saving	% Saving	Pro Time	DIY Time
$1,800	$1,275	$525	30	19	27

INSTALL A FIBERGLASS TUB SURROUND

If the walls surrounding a bathtub have seen better days, you can cover them with a three-panel fiberglass surround that is easy to install and will be easy to maintain for many years. The back panel and two end panels usually have preformed soap dishes, shelves and even a grab bar. The molded panels are easy to clean because there are no tight corners to catch dirt. Since the unit comes in parts it will fit through the bathroom door.

A contractor will charge $260 to install the unit or you can buy one at a home center for $205, install it and save 20 percent. You'll need a carpenter's level, coping saw, hole saw attachment, an electric drill and a caulk gun. Figure it for a five-hour job from start to finish.

You can tackle the job if the walls surrounding the tub are structurally sound. A complication comes up if there's rotten plaster or wallboard and studs, which should be removed and repaired before the new tub surround is installed. An experienced do-it-yourselfer can do it, but it makes the job more difficult and time-consuming.

One tricky part is making the cuts for the faucet valves on the front end panel. It sounds more difficult than it is, because the trim rings will usually hide any small miscuts.

Adhesive holds the panels to the wall and all joints are covered with strips and sealed with caulk. The secret to a good installation is to caulk the joint between the tub and fiberglass panels with a long-lasting silicone caulk.

TIP BOX

When applying caulk, don't pull the caulk nozzle toward you, push it away to force the caulk into the joint. Smooth the surface with a finger wetted in water for a professional-looking finish.

TABLE

Pro Cost	DIY Cost	DIY Saving	% Saving	Pro Time	DIY Time
$260	$205	$55	20	2	5

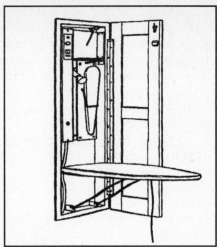

INSTALL AN
IRONING BOARD CUPBOARD

In many older kitchens an iron and ironing board were standard equipment and consequently there was a nifty little cupboard built into a wall. Even with permanent press clothes, an ironing board is still handy to have in a kitchen or laundry area today. You can buy a self-contained ironing board center that is ready to build into a wall cavity for about $250 and install it or pay a contractor $380 to do the job. It's a do-able job if you have some carpentry experience, and you'll pocket a nice 34 percent saving.

When choosing a location for the unit, be sure it's near an electrical receptacle, because it contains a light and electrical receptacle for the iron. If you are not experienced with electrical work, leave this part of the project to an electrician.

Also consider how the unfolded ironing board will affect the floor plan of the room. The wall where you plan to install the unit must be free of plumbing pipes and electrical wires. If it's not, choose another location or hire a contractor to do the job because you'll have to move the plumbing pipes or electrical lines.

Installing the cupboard between the wall studs requires cutting into an existing wall; the trim around the unit conceals the raw opening in the wall so there's no finishing required. Most of the units come complete with fasteners, electrical wires and connectors. You'll need a saw, hammer, drill and screwdriver to do the job. It will take a long afternoon to complete the installation.

The best time to add this cupboard is when you're in the midst of a remodeling job, because the walls are then open and exposed.

TIP BOX

To determine what's behind a wall, use an inexpensive stud finder to make sure that the cavity is hollow.

TABLE

Pro Cost	DIY Cost	DIY Saving	% Saving	Pro Time	DIY Time
$380	$250	$130	34	2	5

REBUILD A WINDOW

To replace a rattling old window, that is loose in its frame, with a new energy-efficient one costs about $250. A less expensive alternative is to rebuild the old window using an aluminum jamb liner kit with weather-stripped channels. A homeowner with some carpentry experience can use this approach, which is especially appealing when several windows need fixing.

You can buy and install a jamb liner kit for a 3-by-4-foot double-hung window for $40 or hire a carpenter to do the job for $110. You cut the jamb liners to fit and install them with the old sashes on the interior sides of the window. They replace the worn out slots where the window sashes slide up and down. The job involves removing the inner and outer window sashes and then the wooden parting stops that holds the sashes in place. Then you remove the sash weight cords and fill the cavities with insulation. The final step is reinstalling the old sashes in the jamb liners and installing the assembly (liners and sashes) back in the window.

You'll save 64 percent by doing it yourself and you'll need these basic tools: hammer, pry bar, screwdriver, hacksaw and paint scraper. It's helpful to have an extra pair of hands when you fit the sashes into the jamb liners and lift the assembly into the window opening. It takes about four hours to do a window.

The retrofit gives you a tightly sealed window that goes up and down easily. The kits come in various sizes and are sold at home centers, lumberyards and glass services.

TIP BOX

If the windows needs a fresh coat of paint, remove the sashes and paint them separately before assembling them in the jamb liners.

TABLE

Pro Cost	DIY Cost	DIY Saving	% Saving	Pro Time	DIY Time
$110	$40	$70	64	3	4

INSTALL AND FINISH RECYCLED WALLBOARD

Wallboard, also called Sheetrock and drywall, is used in just about every remodeling and building project. Hanging it yourself can be tempting because you can save 72 percent of what a rocker or wall-board installer charges. Despite the savings, it's not a good job to tackle yourself for several reasons.

For one thing, it's time- and labor-intensive because the job is spread out over a long period, especially when there's only one person doing it. It takes time and practice to learn the techniques, and just when you get the hang of it (no pun intended), your job is over. The panels are heavy and their corners get crushed easily, so manhandling them is strenuous work. And while the work is under way, it's very messy because of the sanding and subsequent film of grit left to linger in the air and infiltrate the rest of the house.

The one exception is when there's only a small area to cover; it's difficult to get an installer then because the job doesn't pay.

Whether you hire a contractor or do it yourself, choose a new wallboard made of recycled paper. It can be installed with nails, screws or staples; the tapered panel edges are joined with an adhesive compound, and then a topping compound finishes the seam. You can also use tape and compound, but taping isn't required if you use a two-step joint system.

To hang recycled wallboard in a 10-by-12-foot room (400 square feet) an installer will charge $465 or you can buy the materials and do the work for $130. The material is heavier to hang and denser than traditional wallboard and the job will take several days. To install it you'll need a saber saw, drywall screwgun, measuring tape, rafter's square and utility knife.

TIP BOX

Buy plenty of extra blades for the utility knife because the material is harder to cut than standard paper-faced wallboard.

TABLE

Pro Cost	DIY Cost	DIY Saving	% Saving	Pro Time	DIY Time
$465	$130	$335	72	10	27

CHAPTER 3

REPLACE A KITCHEN SINK AND FAUCET

Everyone in the house uses the kitchen sink, so it's an appliance that gets a real workout day in and day out. You can replace a worn or undersized single-bowl sink and faucet with a new two-compartment unit if you have some plumbing experience. You'll find a good-quality double-bowl, stainless steel sink and a stylish high-rise kitchen faucet with a spray attachment at home centers for $250. A plumber will charge $150 to remove the old unit and install a new one, so it'll cost $400 to have the job done. You'll save 38 percent if you do it yourself.

If you decide to tackle the project yourself, choose a new sink that has the same dimensions as the old one so the countertop doesn't have to be modified. A self-rimming stainless sink is the easiest type to install because it comes with clips that slide into a channel welded to the bottom side of the sink. The top of the sink has a wide flange that rests on the countertop.

You can reuse the old faucet and save $50 to $60 if you choose a sink

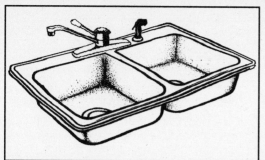

with the same faucet mounting holes as the old one. If the drain traps, pipes and riser pipes that bring water to the faucet are in good shape they should be reused; otherwise replace them.

You'll need these basic tools: slip joint pliers, a screwdriver and an adjustable wrench. The money you save will be well earned because it's a full day of plumbing work that can be challenging, even to those with experience. Your potential savings can literally go down the drain if the sink or faucet leaks and creates water damage.

TIP BOX

Buy a basin wrench (under $10) if you don't have one. It lets you tighten the pipe joints from under the sink, where it's impossible to manipulate a standard wrench.

TABLE

Pro Cost	DIY Cost	DIY Saving	% Saving	Pro Time	DIY Time
$400	$250	$150	38	3	5

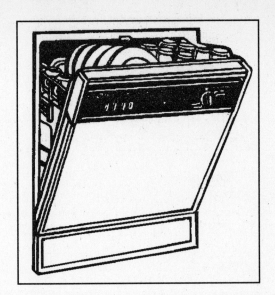

INSTALL A
DISHWASHER

You can't expect a dishwasher to last longer than about ten years, so when the cost of repairing it comes close to the ticket price of a new unit, its time has come. A plumber will charge about $610 to install a new good-quality dishwasher. You can buy one for $440, install it yourself and pocket almost 30 percent savings if you have basic plumbing skills or want to acquire them. The qualifier here is that no changes to the existing plumbing and cabinetry are needed, which is usually the case if your new unit is made by the same manufacturer as the old one.

When the switch involves a change in brand or model, hire a plumber who can deal with moving the water supply, drainpipe or electrical lines, jobs best left for a professional.

If you buy a replacement unit with the water and electrical supply and drain lines in the same location, then you can make the swap. The old owner's manual shows the location of the hookups, so bring it along when you shop for a new one.

The replacement can be done in a day and it's useful to have someone help you muscle the old unit out and the new one in. You'll need only basic plumbing tools: slip joint pliers, adjustable wrench and assorted screwdrivers.

Call your garbage service or town office to find out the best way to dispose of the old unit if you do the job yourself; otherwise the plumber is responsible for removing it. Make arrangements to have the new appliance delivered unless you have a pickup truck or van.

And consider this: You may be better off doing part of the job yourself and hiring a plumber to complete the job. You can remove the old unit and have everything ready so all the plumber has to do is hook up the new unit.

TIP BOX

Protect the floor in front of the dishwasher with heavy cardboard or an old blanket to prevent the old unit from scratching the floor as you push and pull it out from under the countertop.

TABLE

Pro Cost	DIY Cost	DIY Saving	% Saving	Pro Time	DIY Time
$610	$440	$170	28	4	7

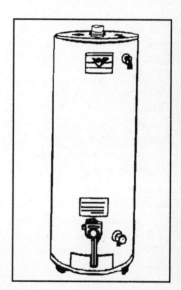

REPLACE A GAS WATER HEATER

More than half of the houses in this country are fueled by natural gas, so the replacement market for gas hot water heaters is a brisk business. To have a tank replaced by a plumber costs almost double what it costs to do it yourself. For example, you can buy an energy-efficient, 40-gallon gas hot water heater and an installation kit with flexible coupling hoses and all the necessary fittings for $275. A plumber charges $520 to install one plus providing the added service of removing the old unit, a big plus unless you have a pickup truck or van.

If you do the job, disconnect and remove the old unit and clean the area before installing the new one. You can reuse the flue pipe from the old heater if it is properly sized to fit the new unit and not too rusty. If a new gas or water line is needed and you're not comfortable or experienced working with pipes, hire a plumber so you'll be assured of a safe installation. Figure the job will take you the better part of a day to complete.

If you have to pay for delivery, make sure the tank is carried to the area where it will be installed. Depending on where you live, you may have to pay a fee to your garbage service or when you take the old unit to your local refuse center. (Getting the rusty old brute out the house is sometimes the most challenging part of the job!)

TIP BOX

Arrange the tank swap when hot water is not needed in the house so it's not an inconvenience to everyone.

The cumbersome old tank can be difficult to manhandle. Try this: Place it on an old blanket, rug or mat and drag it across the floor. Use the same technique outside to prevent scraping the lawn or driveway.

TABLE

Pro Cost	DIY Cost	DIY Saving	% Saving	Pro Time	DIY Time
$520	$275	$245	47	3	7

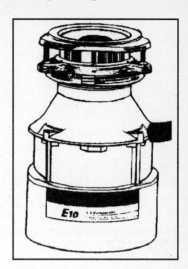

REPLACE A GARBAGE DISPOSAL

A garbage disposal in a kitchen makes short work of dealing with food scraps, so it's a necessary luxury for most of us. Replacing an old unit with a new one is a do-able do-it-yourself project if the plumbing and electrical lines are configured in the same way as the old one. If the replacement involves running new plumbing and electrical lines, it's a job best left to the pro.

You can buy a good quality disposal for about $85 and install it or hire a plumber for $210 to do the job. If you do the job, figure you'll be under the sink for at least half a day and save almost 60 percent for your work. You'll need a screwdriver, slip joint pliers and pipe wrench.

To work comfortably, empty the base cabinet under the sink so you have room to move around. Make an accurate diagram of the plumbing and electrical connections for the old unit or bring the owner's manual when you shop for a replacement. If you can't find an exact replacement, ask for help choosing the necessary plumbing fittings to hook up the new unit to your existing drain line.

Turn off the electricity at the unit and at the main circuit panel, and turn off the water at the stop valves under the sink. Unfasten the old unit, which is probably held in place by a metal ring. Use a screwdriver to loosen the ring and then the unit will drop free of the sink. If a steel band or plate holds it in place, loosen the turnscrews or bolts to free it.

TIP BOX

Some types of disposals are turned on with a switch on the wall which is called continuous feed. Others are activated by placing the drain plug in the unit and they are called batch-type units. To avoid changing the wiring, choose a replacement disposer that matches the old one.

TABLE

Pro Cost	DIY Cost	DIY Saving	% Saving	Pro Time	DIY Time
$210	$85	$125	59	2	4

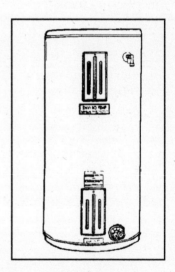

REPLACE AN ELECTRIC WATER HEATER

An electric water heater is easier to install than a gas unit because there's no piping or flue pipe to be concerned about. The heater is basically a large tank containing two electric elements that heat the water. When the elements wear out, they can be replaced, but eventually the tank itself rusts and begins to leak. When this happens, the unit must be replaced.

You can buy a good-quality energy-efficient 40-gallon electric water heater for $230 at most home centers and appliance stores and install it, saving 43 percent of what it costs to have a plumber do the work. A plumber will charge $410 to haul away the old unit and replace it with a new one. Part of this cost is disposing of the old unit, which often involves a disposal fee, to have it picked up and taken to your local refuse center.

Most stores sell electric water heater installation kits, which contain flexible connectors that make it easy to hook the tank to the existing plumbing. The electrical connection is very straightforward and can be done safely by a do-it-yourselfer with little plumbing or electrical experience.

If the pipes and shut-off valves leading to the old water heater are not rusted, they can be reused. Do not reuse the safety valve. If the new heater doesn't come with a pressure relief valve, buy a new one. A plumber can make the swap in half a day, but you should plan on spending more than that to install the new unit yourself.

TIP BOX

You can increase the life of the new water heater by periodically draining the sediment from the bottom of it. Connect a garden hose to the drain valve and empty a few gallons of water from the tank twice a year.

TABLE

Pro Cost	DIY Cost	DIY Saving	% Saving	Pro Time	DIY Time
$410	$230	$180	43	4	7

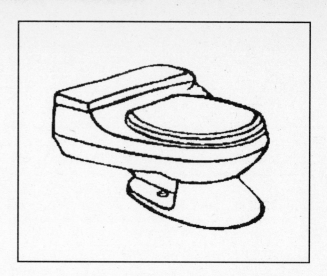

REPLACE A TOILET

The most frequently used water appliance in a house is also one of the most mysterious, yet how it works is quite simple. A typical two-part toilet with a tank and bowl works because of gravity and water pressure. Water falls from the tank into the bowl when the toilet is flushed, and forces the bowl water into the waste line of the plumbing system. New water flows into the tank from a pressurized supply line so the cycle can begin again.

Toilets last for a long time, so most often they are replaced because of remodeling. Newer units may be better looking but they are also designed to use less water. Replacing a toilet is a project that the average handyman can do and the payoff can be a 30 percent savings. For example, you can replace an old toilet with a new high-end low-profile one-piece water-saving toilet for about $400. A plumber will charge about $580 for the job.

Newer toilets are designed to be installed on a drainpipe located 12 inches from the finished wall. This distance is one of the roughing-in measurements used by the plumber to install the toilet. Older toilets may have different roughing-in dimensions, so you have to carefully measure the distance between the back wall and the bolts holding the toilet to the floor. If this measurement is more than 12 inches, a modern toilet can be installed, but it will be slightly farther from the back wall. If the measurement is less than 12 inches, consider hiring a plumber to make the swap or be very sure the new toilet will fit the smaller roughing-in dimensions.

Along with the new toilet, buy a flexible riser tube to connect the new toilet to the water supply, a new wax ring to form a seal between the toilet and the waste pipe and plumber's putty to seal between the toilet bottom and floor. You'll need only basic plumbing tools like an adjustable wrench, a screwdriver, putty knife, hacksaw and a pail and sponge.

TIP BOX

Check with your local building department before you purchase the toilet to see what the specifications are for toilets and their water consumption.

TABLE

Pro Cost	DIY Cost	DIY Saving	% Saving	Pro Time	DIY Time
$580	$400	$180	30	4	4

REPLACE A VANITY AND FAUCET

Upgrading a bathroom with a new vanity and faucet is an improvement you'll appreciate and enjoy every time you use it. And since the bathroom is an important feature of a house when you go to sell it, your improvement won't go unnoticed by a potential buyer. Since the vanity commands much of the floor and wall space in a bathroom, you can dramatically change the look of your bathroom by replacing it.

You can purchase a good-quality, 30-inch-wide cabinet base, topped with a synthetic marble sink, and a new faucet for about $325. If you are an experienced do-it-yourselfer and have done some minor plumbing before, you should be able to complete this project. A plumber will charge just under $500 for the same job. You'll save more than 30 percent if you do it.

It is easiest to replace a vanity with one of the same size or larger. Unless the existing unit was installed after flooring and wallcovering were in place, there will be a gap when a smaller vanity replaces it. Check out the inside compartment of the old vanity to see how it's constructed and where the drain and water supply lines enter. If you plan to do the job, choose a new vanity that is built the same so it doesn't have to be modified to fit over the existing pipes.

This is a full day's job, so schedule your time accordingly. It will take more time and money if additional plumbing work is needed or if the walls or floor need some repair work. To complete this project you'll need these: wide-blade putty knife, adjustable wrench, basin wrench, slip joint pliers and basic carpentry tools.

TIP BOX

If the old vanity is stuck to the wall because of layers of paint, use a wide-blade putty knife to pry it loose. Thoroughly clean the walls and floor when the old vanity has been removed and before installing the new one.

TABLE

Pro Cost	DIY Cost	DIY Saving	% Saving	Pro Time	DIY Time
$495	$325	$170	34	5	9

REPLACE A KITCHEN FAUCET

Nothing beats the convenience of a single-lever faucet at the kitchen sink, because it lets you freely adjust hot and cold water levels. By replacing an old faucet with a new one with a spray attachment, you'll give a quick facelift to the sink and counter and enjoy the convenience.

If you can find a new single-handled faucet that will fit into your sink, this replacement is a do-able job for even a first-time do-it-yourselfer, because there are no additional plumbing lines to run or holes to cut.

The easiest way to see what kind of mounting holes your sink has is to look underneath it. Note how many holes there are and the distance between them and choose a new faucet that fits into these holes. At home centers and plumbing suppliers you'll find good-quality single-lever faucets for about $50. Expect to pay a plumber at least $75 for the faucet and installation. For a few hours work you'll save 34 percent.

You'll need a few basic plumbing tools like a channel-type pliers, an adjustable wrench or basin wrench, a screwdriver and measuring tape. When you are shopping for the faucet, get a set of flexible copper or plastic riser tubes and a small tub of plumber's putty to bed in the base of the new faucet. All faucets come with installation instructions, so take a look at them to make sure you have everything needed to make the swap.

If your plumbing is very old and the pipes under the sink are rusted, it's worth it to hire a plumber, because dealing with old pipes can be a real challenge, even for a seasoned pro. A good plumber will know what to replace and what is still usable, which may save you money in the long run.

TABLE

Pro Cost	DIY Cost	DIY Saving	% Saving	Pro Time	DIY Time
$75	$50	$25	34	1	2

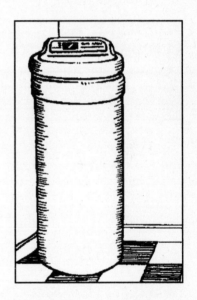

INSTALL A WATER SOFTENER

A home water treatment system is necessary in some parts of the country to balance the water so it's not hardened with excessive deposits of calcium and magnesium. An average-sized water softener can remove up to 50 grains of hardness per gallon of water or 16,500 grains of hardness per regeneration cycle. You can buy a unit at a home center for about $570 and install it if you have experience with plumbing projects. A plumber will charge $800, so you save 29 percent doing it yourself.

This is not a project for the first-time plumber because you have to cut into the main water supply line leading into the house and redirect it to the unit. Treating only the hot water is a good idea since the problems of hardened water show up in the shower, laundry and sink. So if you want to condition only the hot water, you will have to run a new pipe from the water softener to the hot water heater. The softener also needs a drain line run to a laundry sink or floor drain and a 110 volt electrical outlet to run its clock.

Even though much of this work can be done with plastic pipe, which is easier to use than galvanized steel or copper pipe, there is still a lot of cutting and fitting required. It's one of those jobs where it is difficult to anticipate all the different types of pipe fittings that will be needed, so you may spend a good deal of your time running back and forth to the store.

You will need some advanced plumbing tools like a tubing cutter, or maybe even a pipe threader. A plumber has everything needed right on the truck and can usually get the job done in half a day; it takes a homeowner a day and then some. Remember that while you are working on this project, the water will be turned off to the house.

TIP BOX

Sodium is a byproduct of the water softening treatment so a hot-water-only installation is a good choice, especially for people who are on a sodium-restricted diet.

TABLE

Pro Cost	DIY Cost	DIY Saving	% Saving	Pro Time	DIY Time
$800	$570	$230	29	4	9

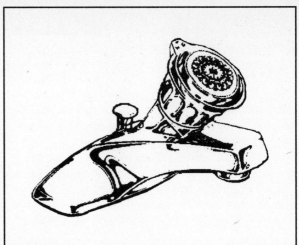

REPLACE A BATHROOM FAUCET

Even though it's a small fixture in the bathroom, it's surprising how a new faucet can update the look of the entire room. Replacing one is a job a first-time plumber can tackle, and save considerably in the process. You can buy a brass, washerless faucet with a pop-up drain and riser tubes for about $85 and install it, saving 35 percent. The job should take a few hours to complete. A plumber will do the job for $130.

It is a good idea to take the old faucet with you when shopping for a replacement. If that's not possible, carefully measure the size and distance between the holes in the sink top to make sure you get a new fixture that fits the existing holes.

You'll need a few basic plumbing tools like an adjustable wrench and a pair of channel-lock pliers. If the vanity is small, buy a $10 basin wrench which allows you to easily reach under there and tighten the riser tubes connecting the faucet to the plumbing. Prevent scratching the new finish by wrapping masking tape around all nuts.

Before beginning, clear out the contents of the vanity cabinet beneath the sink so you'll have working space, and remove anything on top of the countertop.

Don't forget before you begin to turn off the water at the stop valves under the sink or at the main supply.

Some older sinks have separate hot and cold faucets which you can replace with a pair of washerless faucets.

TIP BOX

Before you test the faucets, remove the aerator from the end of the spigot. A load of dirt and mineral sediments will come out. Unclog the screen of the aerator by holding it under a flow of water.

TABLE

Pro Cost	DIY Cost	DIY Saving	% Saving	Pro Time	DIY Time
$130	$85	$45	35	1	3

INSTALL A PEDESTAL SINK

The clean lines of a pedestal sink complement just about any style bathroom. You'll find contemporary designs with thin, streamlined bases or replicas of charming old-fashioned pedestal sinks that are appealing in a country or Victorian decor. A pedestal sink is particularly well suited in tight quarters where space is at a premium, because its narrow base takes up less room than a bulky cabinet.

To have a plumber install a new pedestal sink will cost about $330 or you can buy the sink with the valve and drain fittings for $180 and install it yourself, which is a nice 45 percent savings. It's a do-able job for a homeowner with some plumbing experience.

To determine which sink to buy, consider its style and its rough-in dimensions, which should come close to the existing one. Many older sinks are wall-mounted, with the supply lines close underneath. Some new sinks require that the supply lines be located lower on the wall, so check the dimensions carefully.

If you can find a sink that fits your existing pipe layout, the swap is much easier. You can use flexible chromed copper or PVC plastic risers to connect the water lines. You can also replace the old trap assembly with a plastic one. The job will take the better part of a day and you'll need only basic tools: slip joint pliers, an adjustable wrench and a screwdriver. A basin wrench will make installing the valve easier.

If the sink is not a good fit, you will have to extend, or possibly shorten, the water supply pipes and drain lines. Unless you are experienced working with old pipes, hire a plumber.

> **TIP BOX**
>
> If there are no stop valves under the sink, it's a good time to install them. Stop valves let you turn off the water to the faucet you're working on instead of turning off the water to the whole house.

TABLE

Pro Cost	DIY Cost	DIY Saving	% Saving	Pro Time	DIY Time
$330	$180	$150	45	2	6

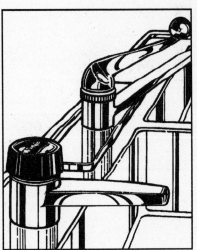

INSTALL A HOT WATER DISPENSER

The grocery stores are stocked with shelves full of dry mixes for hot beverages and soups so a sink-top boiling water dispenser is a handy appliance for today's busy households. To add one requires very little in the way of plumbing experience, so it's a do-able project for just about anyone. You can buy the unit for about $140 and install it or hire a plumber, who will do the job for $200. If you decide to tackle the job, you'll pocket a 30 percent savings for just a few hours.

To accommodate a hand spray many sinks have a precut hole in the back shelf which is ideal for installing a hot water dispenser. All you have to do is remove the cap that plugs the opening and insert the dispenser spigot. Its heater unit mounts under the sink. Most of the hot water dispensers can tap into an existing water line with a saddle valve that clamps over an existing pipe. If a saddle isn't included with the unit, purchase one. If your sink doesn't have a precut hole, the spout can be mounted in a hole cut into the countertop next to the sink. You'll need only basic plumbing tools like channel lock-type pliers or a small pipe wrench, a screwdriver and an electric drill and hole saw if you need to make a hole for the dispenser.

The hot water dispenser requires a source of electricity. If there's a garbage disposal or dishwasher at the sink, you'll find an electrical outlet under the sink that you can use. If the wires run directly to a disposal or dishwasher and there is no outlet, you will have to install one. This is probably a job best left to an electrician since working with electricity around water can be dangerous.

TIP BOX

If you are going to be away for more than a few days, turn off the unit to conserve electricity. You will not save any energy by turning it off overnight.

TABLE

Pro Cost	DIY Cost	DIY Saving	% Saving	Pro Time	DIY Time
$200	$140	$60	30	2	3

CHAPTER
4

INSTALL TRACK
LIGHTING

Track lighting has its origins in the theater, but today it goes center stage in any kind of room. It's effective accenting a piece of art on a wall or on display, providing task lighting over a desk or illuminating a work area in a busy kitchen. It's an attractive alternative lighting style with movable individual heads that give you lighting on demand since they can swivel to focus in any direction and direct light where its needed.

With just basic knowledge of how electricity works in a house, an experienced do-it-yourselfer can install track lighting in a room with an existing overhead lighting fixture. If there's not a ceiling fixture already there, hire an electrician to install the track lighting, because a new electric circuit and wall switch are needed and fishing wires through the wall is best left to a professional.

You can buy a track lighting kit which consists of an 8-foot-long track with six heads and a power attachment module for about $150 and install it yourself, saving almost 30 percent of what an electrician charges. The job involves wiring the track, installing the end and con-

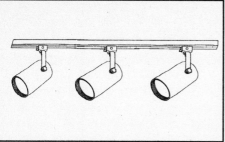

nector fittings to the existing ceiling box and installing the light units. The job should take you about three hours. You'll need a ladder because the work is done overhead, plus a drill, screwdriver and a pair of wire cutters. Be careful because you're working with electricity, and follow the installation instructions supplied with the unit.

If you're intimidated by electrical work, an electrician will charge $210 to do the job; budget about $100 dollars more if a new circuit is needed.

TIP BOX

Don't ever rely on just turning off the electricity at the wall switch. Turn off power at the main circuit panel because there may be other hot wires in the ceiling box not controlled by the wall switch.

TABLE

Pro Cost	DIY Cost	DIY Saving	% Saving	Pro Time	DIY Time
$210	$150	$60	28	1	3

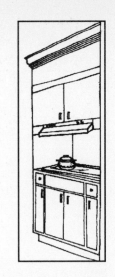

INSTALL A
DUCTLESS STOVE HOOD VENT

When you can smell what's cooking on the stove throughout the house, it's time to consider investing in a stove vent. A ductless hood vent with a light is a good choice because it is easy to install. It provides efficient removal of stovetop odors as well as airborne grease, which damages wallcovering and paint near the stove. The hood mounts easily on the underside of a cabinet over the stove, and since it is vented into the room, you don't have to cut through an exterior wall.

An electrician will charge $275 to install a good-quality 30-inch ductless stove hood. If there's an electrical outlet in the wall near the stove, a homeowner with some electrical experience can tackle this job. You can buy the stove hood for $150, install it and pocket a 45 percent savings.

This project will take you about three hours and you'll need only basic tools: hammer, level, screwdriver, tape measure, drill and wire cutters.

If there is not an electrical outlet near the stove, figure it will take more time to fish some electrical wires through the wall into the cabinet above the vent. If you're at all intimidated by working with electricity, install the vent and then call in an electrician to wire it up.

TIP BOX

A hood unit with an outside vent is more efficient removing odors but much more difficult to install because you have to open an exterior wall to run ducting from the hood to the outside. Budget more time and money if you choose this type of vent.

TABLE

Pro Cost	DIY Cost	DIY Saving	% Saving	Pro Time	DIY Time
$275	$150	$125	45	1	3

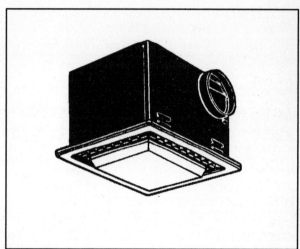

INSTALL A BATHROOM VENT/LIGHT

Most problems with mildew, peeling wallpaper and rotten windowsills in a bathroom are caused by excessive moisture. There are many remedies for these problems, but unless there is proper ventilation, all the moisture problems will eventually return.

Replacing an existing overhead light with a combination vent/light unit will go a long way to solve most moisture problems and it is probably a project most experienced do-it-yourselfers can handle. But there are several qualifiers: If the vent duct for the combination fixture can be run directly through an exterior wall or into an existing attic and if you can use the existing wiring in the ceiling to power the new vent/light, it's a do-able project for do-it-yourselfer. But if the duct has to run through a brick wall or pass through the roof, or if there's no usable wiring in place, hire an electrician because it's a job for someone with more skills than the average homeowner.

For less than $100 you can buy a vent/light fixture with an installation kit, which includes a through-the-wall vent with exhaust hood and 4-inch-diameter flexible duct. You'll need basic carpentry and electrical tools and it will take you a good day's work to complete the job. An electrician will charge $170 to do the job, by doing it yourself you'll save 44 percent.

TIP BOX

Remember wiring in a bathroom requires ground fault protection, and before you begin any work, turn off the electricity to the bathroom at the main panel.

TABLE

Pro Cost	DIY Cost	DIY Saving	% Saving	Pro Time	DIY Time
$170	$95	$75	44	3	7

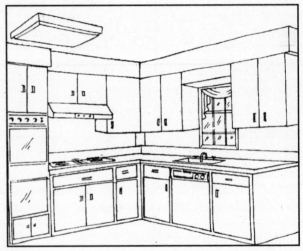

REPLACE A KITCHEN LIGHT

The room in a house that requires the best lighting often has the most inadequate—the kitchen, where you're preparing food with sharp knives, reading and dining. In a newly constructed house, the lighting is often below standard unless you paid for the lighting upgrade package with additional fixtures. And in older homes the typical two-bulb fixture in the center of the ceiling isn't nearly enough lighting.

Even a first-time handyman can replace a ceiling fixture with a three- or four-bulb fluorescent fixture, because you're basically just untwisting and twisting similar wires. It's a simple job for an electrician, so one can do it quickly. The major cost of the project is the fixture itself, about $120 for a 4-foot fluorescent ceiling fixture trimmed in oak. If you supply the labor, you can save about $36 or a quarter of what an electrician charges. It'll take less than two hours and it's helpful to have two people involved so one can work on the wires while the other holds the fixture. You'll need to have a screwdriver, wire cutters, electrical tape and a ladder.

Unpack the fixture carefully and identify the parts. Read through the installation instructions a few times so you're familiar with the process. Before you begin working on any electrical project, at the main service panel turn off the power to the circuit serving the light.

If the new fixture is part of a kitchen facelift and painting is involved, use this approach: Remove the old fixture and pay attention to which wires you untwisted or screws or bolts you loosened. Then paint the ceiling. When it's dry, install the new fixture according to the manufacturer's directions.

TIP BOX

Don't forget to buy the bulbs, because they don't come with the fixture.

TABLE

Pro Cost	DIY Cost	DIY Saving	% Saving	Pro Time	DIY Time
$156	$120	$36	23	1	2

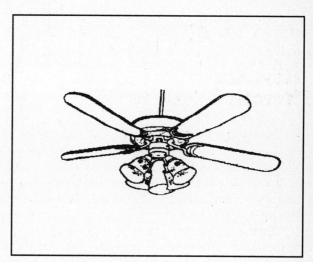

INSTALL A CEILING FAN

From its humble beginnings as a practical way to circulate air in the stuffy Tropics, today's ceiling fan has become a design statement used in every room of the house. The styles run the gamut from high-tech designs in jazzy contemporary colors to old-fashioned Victorian in rich brass and wood. Many of the designs offer add-on light fixture components so a fan can illuminate while cooling a room. If the room has an existing overhead fixture with a wall switch, just about anyone can replace the old light with a ceiling fan.

The cost of fans varies widely, depending on quality and features, but you can expect to pay at least $125 for a good-quality unit. An electrician will charge about $200 to install one, and more if a new electrical line must be run to the ceiling. For a half day's work you'll save 37 percent by doing it yourself.

Securing the fan to the ceiling can be a challenge because many of the ceiling boxes in homes won't carry the weight of the fan, so they must be reinforced or replaced. An installation kit includes a special ceiling box designed for easy installation and capable of supporting the weight of the fan. You'll need these tools to install the fan and installation kit: a screwdriver, hammer, pliers, wire cutters, circuit tester and ladder.

If the fan is equipped with a light, consider installing another switch so you can control the fan and the light separately. The switches are sold as an accessory to the fan.

Always be careful working with electricity, and before doing any electrical work, turn the power off at the circuit panel or fuse box, then test the circuit to make sure that it is dead.

TIP BOX

To balance the paddles tape a metal washer (or a coin) to the top of one paddle. Observe if the fan wobble is less; if not, move the weight from paddle to paddle until the fan runs smoothly.

TABLE

Pro Cost	DIY Cost	DIY Saving	% Saving	Pro Time	DIY Time
$200 ·	$125	$75	37	1	4

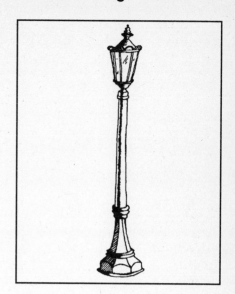

INSTALL A LIGHT POST

A yard lantern is an attractive addition to a house that by lighting the area helps to deter intruders and assures safe footing at night. If you're an experienced do-it-yourselfer, you can tackle this job, but it involves several skills. You have to excavate a hole for the post, then dig a trench for an electrical cable, set the post in concrete and, finally, wire up the lantern.

If the job sounds too complicated and you are intimidated by the electrical work, you can install the post and dig the trench to the house, then hire an electrician to wire up the light, which will save you considerably.

Expect to pay an electrician about $210 to install a good-quality exterior decorative lantern and post that's located less than 30 feet from the house. The post can be either pressured-treated four-by-four lumber or prefabricated metal. The wood post can be set into a hole and backfilled with stone, but the metal post will probably require a concrete pad. If you decide to do the job, it will cost $120 for materials and a day and a half of work. You'll save 43 percent for your efforts.

Before doing anything, check with your building department to see what their requirements are for underground electrical cables. They'll specify how deep you must dig the trench and footings for the post. In most locations the use of direct burial electrical cable is allowed, but not in all areas of the country.

TIP BOX

Consider purchasing a lantern that has a photoelectric eye to turn the light on and off automatically as needed.

TABLE

Pro Cost	DIY Cost	DIY Saving	% Saving	Pro Time	DIY Time
$210	$120	$90	43	4	13

INSTALL A PORCH LANTERN

A porch lantern or coach light at the entry to your house is a welcome sight for visitors when they're looking for your address (or your neighbor's) and it's a good preventive measure against intruders because they prefer a dark entrance where they can't be seen. If the house has an old lantern with wiring already in place a first-time do-it-yourselfer can replace it with a new one without too much difficulty. If new wiring is needed, hire an electrician because this job requires running an electrical line from the main power panel to the porch.

For $45 you can buy a prewired, 60-watt porch lantern for mounting on an outside wall. There are many styles, which are designed to be installed on the siding alongside the door, over the door or in the ceiling of a porch or overhang. For a little more you can purchase a light with a built-in sensor that will turn on when it gets dark and off again in the morning.

You'll need basic electrical tools such as a pair of wire cutters, a screwdriver and electrical tape. Plan on spending a few hours with the hookup.

An electrician will charge about $65 for this small job. So when you do it yourself there's a 30 percent savings.

TIP BOX

Turn off the power to the branch serving the porch. If you are not sure which branch that is, turn off the main power. Tell everyone in the household they'll be without power while you do the job.

TABLE

Pro Cost	DIY Cost	DIY Saving	% Saving	Pro Time	DIY Time
$65	$45	$20	30	1	2

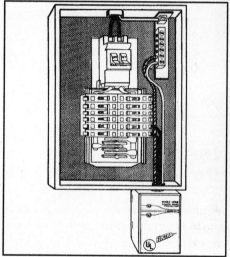

INSTALL A
CIRCUIT PANEL SURGE PROTECTOR

Today's homes are filled with expensive home electronics like computers, microwave ovens, VCRs and CD players, which are all sensitive to voltage spikes. These very short bursts of high voltage are caused by lightning and other surges traveling over the power lines. Even though most surges are minor and will not destroy equipment, they will shorten the life of any electronic component.

To protect home electronics add to your main circuit panel a surge protector which will absorb excess voltage caused by a power surge and allow only normal voltage to pass through to your valuable equipment.

An electrician will charge about $145 to install a circuit panel surge protector, but you can do it yourself in a few hours for $85, saving 40 percent. The unit comes with complete instructions but some electrical know-how is needed to understand how it works. You need these tools:

screwdriver and wire cutters. Before you begin, use an inexpensive neon circuit tester to test that the wires you're working on are dead.

Don't forget that there is always live power inside the main panel, so before you remove the panel cover, turn the power off at the main circuit breaker. Then be very careful not to work near the area where the main power cables enter the box. The surge protector must be wired to the neutral bus bar and one of the circuit breakers, so there is little danger if the power is off.

> **TIP BOX**
>
> Individual, plug-in surge protectors are also useful for additional protection for home electronics like computers.

TABLE

Pro Cost	DIY Cost	DIY Saving	% Saving	Pro Time	DIY Time
$145	$85	$60	41	1	2

WIRE A PHONE EXTENSION

This is a project you can't afford not to do, because it's easy and very inexpensive. Even for a small job like wiring up a phone extension, most telephone companies have a minimum service call charge, which is about $80, even if the extension only uses 20 feet of wire. To do it yourself all you need is about $12 worth of materials—available at home centers, hardware stores and electronic outlets—and an hour or so of your time.

The wire serving a telephone has very low voltage running through it, so there is no shock hazard. Almost all new phones use a modular plug which installs right over the end of the wire, so you don't have to strip any wires. Find a phone jack to tap into to start the wiring of the new extension. If it's a modular jack (one that takes a little plug), your job will be very easy. An older-style jack may need an adapter before it will be compatible with the modular plugs.

You'll need a spool of four-conductor phone wire if the wire will run through walls or in the attic; otherwise, pick up four-conductor modular cable and a surface-mounted modular wall jack. If you are using modular cable, pick up a crimping tool (under $10) which makes it easy to install the plugs. All these materials come in packages with complete installation instructions. You'll probably spend more time shopping for the materials than actually hooking up the new extension.

TIP BOX

Get an inexpensive line tester to verify that everything is hooked up correctly. Plug the tester into the jack, and if the green light comes on, everything is OK. If not, reverse the wires on the terminals.

TABLE

Pro Cost	DIY Cost	DIY Saving	% Saving	Pro Time	DIY Time
$80	$12	$68	85	1	1

CHAPTER
5

INSTALL AN
ATTIC FAN

One of the best ways to cool off a house on a hot summer night is with an attic fan that pulls outside air into the house and pushes warm air out through the attic. These fans are more economical to operate than an air conditioner, so cooling costs will be lowered. You can buy a good-quality 30-inch variable speed fan with a shutter cover and switch for about $195 and install it if you have basic carpentry and electrical skills and tools.

A electrician will charge $465 to do the job. For a weekend's work you'll pocket nearly a 60 percent savings.

Most attic fans are designed for installation in a ceiling without cutting the joists. You still have to cut a hole in the ceiling, but you don't have to make any structural changes in the framing.

You'll need two people involved in this project: someone in the attic cutting the ceiling and another to catch the cutout. There's more team work involved because you'll need help muscling the brute to the attic, while a helper lifts and positions the fan in place and then while it's being attached to the floor joists.

For the fan to operate efficiently there have to be sufficient attic

vents to allow the large volume of air pumped into the attic by the fan to escape. The exact amount of ventilation area required will be noted in the specification sheet supplied by the fan manufacturer. These vents are best located in the upper third of the roof area.

TIP BOX

Plan ahead and schedule this project when working in the attic is comfortable, not during the hot summer months.

TABLE

Pro Cost	DIY Cost	DIY Saving	% Saving	Pro Time	DIY Time
$465	$195	$270	58	4	11

CAULK WINDOWS

Research shows that if you added up all the small cracks and crannies where air leaks into houses built before 1980, you'd have a gap equivalent to two square feet of open area. That's like leaving a small window open all year long—it's a lot of wasted energy!

The gap around windows is one of the major culprits. Air leakage occurs where the frame of the window meets the siding and through wobbly window sashes that don't seal tightly. A painter will charge you $65 to caulk five average-sized windows, which is about 50 to 75 cents a linear foot. But you can do it yourself for $16 worth of materials, the cost of some good acrylic caulk and a caulk gun. For a few hours of work you'll be rewarded with a 75 percent savings.

To do the job correctly you'll need a scraper to remove the old caulk and loose paint. Don't skimp on the quality of caulk you use. Most of the cost of this project is labor, so to get the most return on your efforts choose a top-quality acrylic/latex or acrylic/silicone caulk, which costs between $3 and $5 a tube.

The preparation work is the most time-consuming part of the job because the actual caulking, or laying a bead of caulk, goes quickly. The more you prepare the surface so it's smooth, the better-looking the results. Hold the caulk gun at a 45-degree angle to the crack and apply the caulk by pushing the nozzle instead of pulling it over the crack. Run a wet finger over the wet caulk to smooth it and make it uniform.

TIP BOX

Avoid caulking when the temperature is below 50 degrees.

TABLE

Pro Cost	DIY Cost	DIY Saving	% Saving	Pro Time	DIY Time
$65	$16	$49	75	1	3

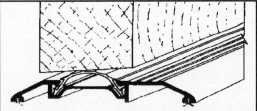

REPLACE A
DOOR THRESHOLD

The bottom of an exterior door is hardly a point of interest, but it should be come wintertime, when it can be a major source of cold air drafts. Your heating costs go up as cold air leaks in, so sealing the door more tightly is money in your pocket. A door threshold is one way to stop the leak. It's an aluminum strip with a vinyl insert that is installed at the bottom of the door. When the door is closed its bottom touches the vinyl insert in the threshold and forms a tight-fitting gasket that stops air infiltration.

You can buy a threshold for about $20 and install it in a few hours or hire a carpenter who charges about $60, so you'll save more than half by doing it yourself. Either way, you'll probably recoup the cost of the threshold in one heating season, so it's a win-win situation, no matter who does the job.

Choose a threshold that is self-adjusting so it can be lowered and raised to accommodate an uneven sill, which is often the case in an older house. You'll need basic carpentry skills and tools. Remove the existing threshold if there is one and clean the area. Follow the manufacturer's directions to install the new one. To completely seal the new threshold tuck fiberglass insulation underneath it and use the screws provided to attach it to the sill.

If you have to cut the bottom of the door so it clears the new threshold, angle the cut slightly so the inside edge of the door is slightly lower than the front outside edge. This lets the door open and close easily. Seal the bare wood with paint or varnish so it won't warp.

TIP BOX

Seal the joints between the threshold and the side of the doorjamb with caulk.

TABLE

Pro Cost	DIY Cost	DIY Saving	% Saving	Pro Time	DIY Time
$60	$20	$40	67	1	3

UPGRADE ATTIC INSULATION WITH FIBERGLASS BATTS

Upgrading your attic insulation is time and money well spent because it will pay back in energy savings for years to come. There should be at least six inches of loose fill insulation between the floor joists to combat weather extremes, so if it's not there, make this job a top priority. Use new poly-wrapped batts that don't itch. You install by simply laying them over the loose fill insulation.

An insulation contractor will charge $790 to install 1,200 square feet of 15-inch-wide, 6¼-inch thick poly-wrapped fiberglass batts. You can buy the insulation and install it yourself for $360, saving more than 50 percent. It's a long day's work and it goes faster if you have a helper so one person can measure and install, while the other cuts the insulation to size.

The job can be tiring if you're not used to physical work, because it involves crawling and stooping in confined areas of the attic and making several trips up and down the attic stairs.

To lay the poly-wrapped insulation in place use these guidelines: If the cavity between the floor joists is not filled to the top of the joists with loose fill insulation, lay the poly-wrapped insulation running in the same direction as the floor joists or parallel to them. If the loose fill insulation fills the cavity between the joists, lay the poly-wrapped insulation perpendicular to the joists.

To measure the batts use a measuring tape and to cut them use a straightedge and a pair of heavy-duty scissors or a utility knife. Wear a long-sleeved shirt, pants, a hat and knee pads. Invest in a good-quality respirator with replaceable filters and safety goggles to protect you from the fiberglass dust.

TIP BOX

Buy a pair of knee pads and you'll spare yourself some sore knees from kneeling on the floor joists.

TABLE

Pro Cost	DIY Cost	DIY Saving	% Saving	Pro Time	DIY Time
$790	$360	$430	54	6	9

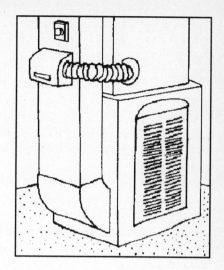

INSTALL A FURNACE HUMIDIFIER

Every winter, as heating systems kick in, homeowners wonder if the cost of heating will remain the same as the year before or if it's likely to be more. One thing you can do to lower heating costs is install a humidifier to your furnace, because as moisture is added to the air, it feels warmer and you can set your thermostat a little lower.

A heating contractor will charge $245 to do the job and an experienced do-it-yourself can buy the unit for $140 and install it, saving more than 40 percent.

Before buying one, check to see that it will fit into the hot air plenum of the furnace. All units come with instructions and provide a template for cutting the mounting hole. They require a water supply, and some need a source of electrical power.

Along with basic tools you'll need a pair of tin snips; the compound leverage-type snips will make cutting easier. To get a supply of water for the humidifier, mount a saddle on a cold water pipe that's near the furnace. This adapter allows you to tap into a pipe without having to cut it.

This is a five-hour job, but one that's worth the effort because, along with lowering your thermostat (and heating bill), you'll no longer have to deal with static-filled dry air during the heating season.

TIP BOX

If possible use unsoftened water for the humidifier. Salt deposits left by water from a softener cause a buildup inside the humidifier.

TABLE

Pro Cost	DIY Cost	DIY Saving	% Saving	Pro Time	DIY Time
$245	$140	$105	43	3	5

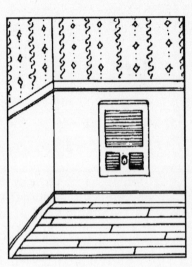

INSTALL AN ELECTRIC WALL HEATER

If you're remodeling and the project involves adding heat to an enclosed porch or room addition, consider using an electric wall heater, which is a wall-mounted unit that provides heat on demand. Most of the time it's less expensive to install a stand-alone unit than to extend your existing central heating system. This may not be the case if your existing system has the extra capacity and there is a heating duct that can be tapped into close to the addition. Electric space heaters are usually more costly to operate than central heating, but units wired for 220 volts are efficient.

You can buy a good-quality 2,000-watt heater for less than $140 and install it if you have some experience working with electricity. It'll take you a good day's work. Otherwise you'll pay an electrician $330 to do the job, which is almost 60 percent more.

Before you do anything, check with your local building department for wiring code requirements. Space heaters draw so much current that they will usually overload an existing house circuit if they are wired to it. So most codes will require that a space heater be on a separate circuit. Follow the code specifications to assure a safe installation.

If you're intimidated by electrical work, hire an electrician to rough in a new circuit to the area where the heater will be installed. Then you install the heater in the wall and complete any carpentry work required.

TIP BOX

The best location for a wall heater is away from a door in the central part of the room, mounted low on the wall.

TABLE

Pro Cost	DIY Cost	DIY Saving	% Saving	Pro Time	DIY Time
$330	$140	$190	58	4	10

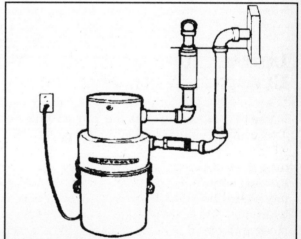

INSTALL A CENTRAL VACUUM SYSTEM

If you've ever lived in a house with a central vacuum system, you'll never be without one. It eliminates dragging heavy equipment up and down stairs and looking for an electrical outlet to power it. You can have a contractor install a central built-in vacuum system for $1,110 or install it yourself for $680. The system typically includes the power unit, PVC tubing and fittings, automatic switch-operated wall inlets, 20 feet of flexible hose and a suction handle with attachments.

The power unit is wall-mounted away from the living area and connected by permanently installed in-wall tubing and fittings. In a one-story or split-level house, mount the unit in the garage, and in a two-story house, install it in the utility area of the basement. A system of branch and inlet lines are connected to the power unit. The tubing is connected to suction outlets located in the walls. It is easy to cut with a handsaw and all joints are glued together. To cut the holes through the flooring and walls for the pipe, rent a reciprocating saw for about $10 a day. You can use a keyhole saw but it will be a difficult job.

This is a time-intensive job that will run several days and can become complicated if obstructions in the walls are discovered. Despite almost a 40 percent savings it's the kind of job that should be left to a professional if there's any doubt in your mind.

If the vacuum system is for a new house under construction, the task becomes far less complicated because the tubing can be run before the walls are put up.

TIP BOX

Plan the run of tubing to be as straight as possible and start its installation at the farthest inlet and work toward the power unit. Secure the tubing to joists or studs so it doesn't sag.

TABLE

Pro Cost	DIY Cost	DIY Saving	% Saving	Pro Time	DIY Time
$1,110	$680	$430	38	13	28

Add Six Inches of Loose-Fill Cellulose Insulation

When you add insulation to an unfinished attic, you're a two-time winner. You save by doing it yourself and you save every month because of lower heating bills. Blowing in six inches of loose-fill cellulose insulation is one of the easiest ways to increase the R-value, or insulating power, in an unfinished attic, because no skills are needed. It's a no-brainer.

An insulation contractor will charge $360 to blow in enough insulation to cover 600 square feet of attic area at least 6 inches deep. If you do the job yourself, you'll save almost 70 percent. Your out-of-pocket cost is $120 for the insulation. The material is bulky, so it's worth a small delivery charge unless you have a van or station wagon to transport it.

To blow the cellulose bags of insulation, you can rent or borrow an insulation blower from the retailer who sells the materials. Or you can simply pour the material straight out of the bags into the cavities between the floor joists. Use a garden rake or broom to spread it around and a yardstick or short pole to coax it into difficult-to-reach areas. Leave it loose, not packed down.

It's a good day's work and you'll be tired from stooping and crawling around the attic, so expect to have some aching joints and muscles when this job is done. Wear a long-sleeved shirt, heavy slacks and shoes, a hat or scarf, a good-quality respirator for lung protection and knee pads for your shins.

> **TIP BOX**
>
> Use a quarter sheet of plywood, which measures two-by-four feet, to span the floor joists as a work platform.

TABLE

Pro Cost	DIY Cost	DIY Saving	% Saving	Pro Time	DIY Time
$360	$120	$240	67	5	9

CHAPTER
6

REPLACE A
SUMP PUMP

You rarely think about a sump pump, but you do notice when it stops working and pumping unwanted water from a crawl space or basement. A sump pump begins pumping as the water level rises in the well or sump that it sits in. Then when the water drains out, the pump turns off. Since a sump pump runs unattended, it can go unserviced, and like any mechanical device, it will eventually wear out and fail. When that happens, you can buy a good-grade submersible ⅓ horsepower sump pump for about $100 and replace it yourself or call a plumber, who'll charge about $200.

It's a do-able job for most homeowners, which saves you half of what the plumber charges. To make the swap as easy as possible take the old pump to the store so you can buy a replacement pump that will fit the existing plumbing. Also replace any rusty or corroded pipes or fittings.

The job will take about two hours from start to finish. Unplug the pump and unscrew the unit from the drainpipe. Most pumps are at-

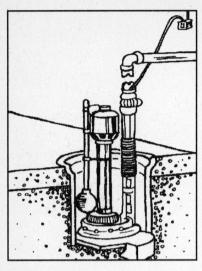

tached to a coupling and can be removed from the drainpipe without cutting it. Pay attention to how the pump comes out, because you'll need to reinstall it in the reverse order. If your pump doesn't have a fitting, you may have to cut the pipe to get the pump out of the sump. If that's the case, buy plastic pipe fittings to reinstall the pump. You'll need a medium-sized pipe wrench or large slip joint type pliers, screwdriver and possibly a hacksaw to complete job.

TIP BOX

Submersible-type sump pumps are less expensive and easier to install than pumps mounted on a pedestal.

TABLE

Pro Cost	DIY Cost	DIY Saving	% Saving	Pro Time	DIY Time
$195	$95	$100	51	1	2

CLEAN A CHIMNEY

Creosote builds up on the interior lining of a chimney and it looks like tar. If there's more than an eighth of an inch buildup, it should be removed to prevent it from causing a fire within the chimney. Cleaning a chimney is not difficult work, but it is messy and requires climbing around on the roof, which is not a job for everyone.

You can hire a chimney sweep to clean a chimney in a typical two-story house for about $70. You can tackle the job yourself for about $20, which is the cost of renting rods and brushes at a rental center. The rods connect together to fit the height of your chimney. To buy, the equipment costs about $10 per six-foot length of rod and the brushes vary from $15 to $40 depending on their diameter.

You need a heavy-duty shop vacuum to suck out the debris, and drop cloths to protect the area around the hearth. Of course, you need a ladder long enough to reach the top of the chimney, or at least to get you on the roof.

It doesn't matter who does the work, the bottom line is that leaving a chimney dirty is dangerous. A bird's nest blocking the flue will fill your house with smoke the first time you try to light a fire, but a buildup of creosote and soot can go unnoticed until you have a roaring chimney fire that could burn your house down.

As long as someone's up on the roof, inspect the chimney to make sure there are no loose bricks. If you find them, repoint them yourself or have it done professionally. Also check to see that the roof shingles are in place.

TIP BOX

Secure drop cloths with heavy tape around the fireplace hearth so the soot doesn't escape into the room when you're cleaning the chimney.

TABLE

Pro Cost	DIY Cost	DIY Saving	% Saving	Pro Time	DIY Time
$70	$20	$50	71	1	2

SECURE A SAGGING CEILING

The thought of tearing out and replacing a cracked or sagging plaster ceiling is not a pleasant one, because when the ceiling is removed, the accumulation of dirt and dust concealed behind it fills the room. A better choice is to reinforce the old cracked plaster ceiling with plaster washers and then laminate drywall on top to create a new surface. The washers stabilize the plaster so a new surface can be installed on top of it.

For a 10-by-12-foot room with 120 square feet of ceiling, you can do the job for about $50, the cost of plaster washers and four sheets of half-inch drywall, or pay a drywall installer $200. You'll save almost 75 percent by doing the work yourself, so it's an appealing job for a handy homeowner to tackle. The project eats up a lot of time, a good long weekend, because of the steps involved and drying time needed for the joint compound.

The job involves preparing the room by moving furniture into clusters so you can move a ladder around the room to reach the ceiling. Protect the furnishings with a lightweight drop cloth and remove all the wall hangings from the wall so dust doesn't settle on top of them. If there's ceiling moulding around the room, remove it using a pry bar. Also remove the light fixture.

Inspect the ceiling for soft areas, where you'll install the washers to secure the loose plaster to the lath behind it. You'll need an electric screw gun with a Phillips head tip to install the washers. Use 2½-inch drywall screws spaced about 6 inches apart around the perimeter of the loose plaster.

When the areas of loose plaster feel tight, hang half-inch drywall over the old plaster with at least 2-inch drywall screws. Then finish the joints with joint tape and compound, and sand smooth.

TIP BOX

Before painting the new drywall, apply a primer designed for treating it so the paint will go on evenly.

TABLE

Pro Cost	DIY Cost	DIY Saving	% Saving	Pro Time	DIY Time
$200	$50	$150	75	18	27

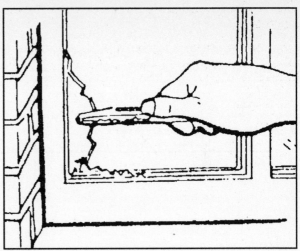

REPAIR
WINDOW GLASS

If anyone in your neighborhood (or family) is a budding all-star there's a good chance someday a baseball or football will come soaring through a window, shattering the glass. If the window is permanent and you can't remove it, you have the choice of hiring a carpenter to make the repair or fixing it yourself. If the broken glass is in a removable window sash or a storm window, you have a third option—take the panel to a hardware store or glass shop and have them replace it.

Hiring a carpenter to make a house call for such a small repair is a nuisance job, so you'll probably be charged a minimum fee of $25 to cover the carpenter's overhead and expenses. You can repair the window yourself and pocket a hefty savings.

You'll need a small box of glazier points, some glazing putty and replacement glass, which will run about $13 for an average-sized window. If the broken glass is in a door, many building codes require that it be replaced with shatterproof plastic or tempered glass, not standard window glass.

Wear work gloves and eye protection and carefully remove the broken pieces of glass from the sash. Use a church key type can opener to clean out the groove that holds the glass and remove the old putty and glazier points. Then measure the length and width for the replacement glass.

Buy a piece of replacement glass to fit the sash and insert it into the window. Then use the tip of a screwdriver to push the glazier points into the sash to hold the glass in place. Form the glazing putty into a rope by rolling it between your hands and then push it into the edge of the sash against the glass. Trim away excess with a putty knife.

TIP BOX

If yours is an odd-shaped window, such as an octagon, make a cardboard template and take it with you when ordering the glass.

TABLE

Pro Cost	DIY Cost	DIY Saving	% Saving	Pro Time	DIY Time
$25	$13	$12	48	½	1

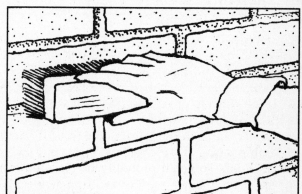

CURE BRICK EFFLORESCENCE

The white powdery blotches that you see on the brick or stone veneer of a house are crystallized salt that has weeped out from the interior. It looks like it was sprinkled randomly on the exterior walls and it's known as efflorescence. This blotchy condition is caused by moisture from within rising to the surface and then evaporating and leaving deposits of mineral salts.

It's not harmful, but you should check out where the moisture is coming from, because if it's the result of water drainage or leaking, it could be more costly if it's not stopped. It might be caused by loose gutters or downspouts that pour rainwater down the brick. Leaking windows that need new caulking are another possibility.

To remove efflorescence from an 8-by-12-foot brick surface, which is roughly 100 square feet, you can hire a contractor, who will charge $75, or do it yourself for $20, saving yourself 73 percent. You need a stiff-bristle wire brush and a garden hose and water.

For a bad stain, rent a power washer for about $50 a day or use muriatic acid mixed with water according to directions. If you use acid, wear rubber gloves and be sure to use eye protection. Flush the area with water after cleaning, and when it is completely dry, apply a water sealer. But before you go out and spend a bundle on rental equipment, be sure to get a bid from a contractor; they already own the equipment and may be less expensive in the long run.

TIP BOX

Because of the high moisture content in freshly applied mortar, new brick houses sometimes develop a white dusty surface. This is from the water in the mortar that has evaporated on the face of the brick and it will disappear as it weathers.

TABLE

Pro Cost	DIY Cost	DIY Saving	% Saving	Pro Time	DIY Time
$75	$20	$55	73	2	3

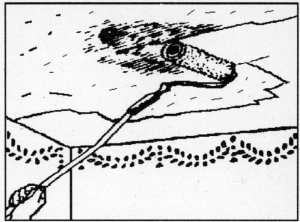

PAINT A STAINED CEILING

Nothing calls unwanted attention in a room more than a blotchy stain on the ceiling, because no matter how lovely it is decorated, a stained ceiling is an eyesore. Anyone who can swing a paintbrush and roller can repair the damage for a fraction of what a painting contractor charges. You can buy the materials needed and make the repair for $30, compared with the $75 a painting contractor would charge. That's a 60 percent savings you can earn in a few short hours of work.

The materials include the cost of a quart of a stain-killing primer-sealer, ceiling paint and a paintbrush, roller and pan. The primer-sealer is a pigmented shellac that holds back the stain so it won't bleed through, and primes the surface so it's ready to paint. You'll also need to have some drop cloths, masking tape, a ladder and household ammonia mixed with water to clean the brush and roller of the primer-sealer.

Spread the drop cloths (old sheets, blankets or plastic sheeting) so the floor and furnishings are protected from paint splatters. Use masking tape at the top of the wall, where it meets the ceiling, to protect the wall from paint splatters. Then paint the stained area with the primer-sealer, using a brush to outline the stain and the roller for large areas. For a small stain, the primer-sealer is available in a spray can. Allow it to dry for about 10 minutes, then recoat if the stain is still visible and let it dry for at least 30 minutes.

Repaint the ceiling with a good-quality flat latex ceiling paint.

TIP BOX

A paint pole that fits into the end of the roller handle makes short work of painting a ceiling.

TABLE

Pro Cost	DIY Cost	DIY Saving	% Saving	Pro Time	DIY Time
$75	$30	$45	60	2	4

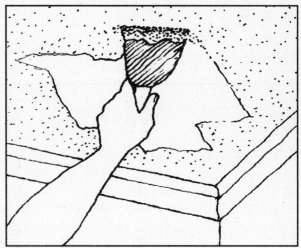

REMOVE TEXTURED PAINT

It is possible to remove textured paint without sanding and scraping. Instead use a textured paint remover available at paint stores and home centers. Removing a heavy layer of textured paint is a messy, labor-intensive job that is a good example of sweat equity. You put in the hard work and you'll be rewarded with a handsome savings.

Apply the remover with a brush, roller or spray gun and wait for it to penetrate and soften the finish. Then scrape it off like jelly. A contractor will charge $340 to do the job. You can buy what you need for $45, do it yourself and save almost 90 percent.

For a typical ceiling in a 12-by-15-foot room (180 square feet), you'll use a gallon of remover, a 4-inch wide-blade putty knife, a half-inch nap roller cover, a roller handle and paint pan. Get an extension pole for the handle or work from a ladder.

Prepare the room by putting the furniture in clusters you can easily move and covering them with heavy drop cloths. To prevent the remover from getting on the ceiling trim or walls, apply a heavy masking tape at the top of the wall around the perimeter of the room, where the wall meets the ceiling.

Figure the job will take a long day's work from start to finish.

TIP BOX

To test whether the paint will be easy or difficult to remove, tape a sponge soaked in rubbing alcohol to the surface. If the finish doesn't soften in ten minutes, it will not be easy to remove.

TABLE

Pro Cost	DIY Cost	DIY Saving	% Saving	Pro Time	DIY Time
$340	$45	$295	87	8	10

CHAPTER
7

INSTALL A
STORM DOOR

It doesn't matter what time of year it is, a combination storm door and interchangeable screen and window panels is an important part of every house. In the hot summer months the screen keeps out pesky mosquitoes and gnats, and come wintertime the window panel keeps cold drafty air from penetrating inside. These doors have never been easier to install, because they are sold as a prehung unit with the hinge and outside mounting flange attached to the door.

For a good-quality, painted aluminum storm/screen door you'll pay $195; a contractor will charge $245 for the door and installation. You can buy it, install it in less than a day and save 20 percent.

To measure the opening for a door, get the inside dimension between the doorjambs and the height of the opening. Choose a door that comes with a door closer and safety chain, which are necessary to prevent the door from being blown open and damaged by strong wind.

Before installing or having installed, check out the doorjamb to see if repair work or a new paint job is needed. Install the new door after the

work has been completed, especially the painting, which is easier to do without the door in place. Budget more time and money for this work.

After installation, run a bead of acrylic latex caulk around the perimeter of the door frame to fill in any gaps. You'll need these tools to hang the door: electric drill, screwdriver, hacksaw, measuring tape, level and caulk gun.

TABLE

Pro Cost	DIY Cost	DIY Saving	% Saving	Pro Time	DIY Time
$245	$195	$50	20	2	5

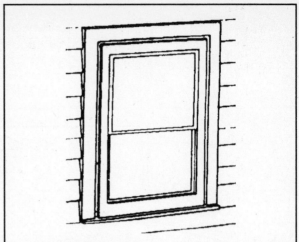

INSTALL AN ALUMINUM STORM WINDOW

The addition of an aluminum storm window helps to keep cool air inside during the summer months when the air conditioner is going, and in the winter heating season it plugs up costly air leakage. A homeowner can install one and save 45 percent of what a contractor charges. However, if the job involves several windows, it's a different story because the economy of numbers works in the contractor's favor and you're better off hiring a professional who can do it cheaper by the dozen.

Even a beginning do-it-yourselfer can install a single storm window, which will cost $55 for an average-sized top-quality unit with a retractable screen and glass panel. A window company will charge almost double, about $100 to make the installation.

It should take less than two hours to install the unit and you'll need some basic carpentry tools, such as a hammer, an electric drill and a carpenter's level.

Get specific instructions from the supplier about exactly which measurements are needed to place the order. Be careful to measure the size accurately because the windows are custom-made and a perfect fit is important if they are to work correctly.

If you're intimidated about working on a ladder and the window is on the second story, it might be worth it to have the work done by the pro.

TIP BOX

If you plan to paint the window frame, do it before hanging the new storm window. Scrape the surface and use a primer on any bare wood, and then paint with an oil-based alkyd exterior paint.

TABLE

Pro Cost	DIY Cost	DIY Saving	% Saving	Pro Time	DIY Time
$100	$55	$45	45	1	2

INSTALL A TV ANTENNA

For a TV or VCR to produce the best picture it must be connected to a good antenna, such as a high-definition one, which improves reception and eliminates the annoying scratchy, snow-filled screen. The antenna can be attached to a house in several locations, such as the roof, chimney or side, or it can hang from rafters or trim boards.

You can buy a mid-range antenna, mast, chimney mount and coaxial cable for $175 and install it yourself or hire a contractor, who will charge $235. If you do it yourself, you'll spend the better part of a day and for your effort save about 25 percent.

Despite the savings, working on a roof is not for everyone, so don't think twice about having a professional do the job if you're concerned about it. If your house has a steeply pitched roof, forget about the savings, and hire an antenna installer who has the training and equipment.

If you do it yourself, you'll need basic electrical tools like a pliers, an adjustable wrench, wire cutters and a crimper to attach the TV coaxial cable fittings to the end of the lead-in cable.

No matter who does the job, plan to have someone in the house watching the television to determine the best reception as someone on the roof slowly turns the antenna and points it toward the television stations you want to receive. In some areas you may need a rotator so you can control the position of the antenna from inside the house for the best reception from stations that are widely separated.

TIP BOX

If you plan on attaching more than one TV to the antenna, use a signal splitter to divide the incoming TV signals between the two sets.

TABLE

Pro Cost	DIY Cost	DIY Saving	% Saving	Pro Time	DIY Time
$235	$175	$60	25	2	6

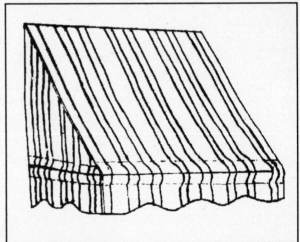

INSTALL A
CANVAS WINDOW AWNING

Whether it's installed on a charming old bungalow or contemporary ranch, a canvas window awning is an attractive addition. It combines practical protection against damaging sun rays and the addition of a dash of color to the exterior of a house. There are ready-made standard-sized canvas awnings sold at home centers and building material suppliers. Or you can order custom-made awnings for odd-sized windows from a canvas shop.

You can have a good-quality standard-sized three-foot-wide canvas awning installed by a professional for $100 or you can buy the awning and install it yourself for $65, saving 35 percent.

Most awnings are held in place by a couple of brackets screwed to the siding or window trim, which hold the top of the frame in place. Depending on whether the awning folds or not, the sides are secured by folding arms or brackets similar to those at the top. In either case, mounting the brackets is not difficult.

To fasten an awning to a brick house, use lead shields to anchor the hardware. Insert the shields into holes drilled into the brick with a masonry drill bit and then install the mounting screws into the lead shield.

Even though installing the awning is very straightforward, plan on spending a few hours on the job. You'll need some basic hand tools like a hammer, drill, screwdriver, an adjustable wrench and two ladders.

Most awnings are sold with the necessary mounting hardware, but if you are buying a custom awning, make sure you get the hardware and fasteners required.

TIP BOX

Get help from someone with a ladder when you raise and position the awning frame against the building. The frame is lightweight, but it can be awkward to handle, especially on a windy day.

TABLE

Pro Cost	DIY Cost	DIY Saving	% Saving	Pro Time	DIY Time
$100	$65	$35	35	1	3

INSTALL A NEW GARAGE ROOF

The savings are too tempting to pass up—but don't be fooled and think laying a new roof is an easy project to do yourself. Even though you can save almost 70 percent, don't do roofing. It's not only difficult, it's dangerous work. Hauling heavy shingles up a ladder is strenuous, and working on a roof is only for a few agile, carpentry-savvy homeowners.

A small job like a simple one-story rancher or a garage roof, however, is do-able for an experienced homeowner. If you want to consider a roofing job, here's how the numbers break down. To install a roof on a 600-square-foot garage requires six squares of shingles (one square covers 100 square feet of roof), roofing paper, nails, aluminum edging and flashing. Using 300-pound fiberglass shingles, the cost of the materials is $260 and a roofer will charge $820 to do the job.

The job will take three long days of your labor, and if there are several layers of old shingles to remove first, it will take even longer. Of course, then your savings will be more because the more labor you invest, the less money you're paying someone else.

To do the job yourself you need basic carpentry tools, a "shingling" or claw hatchet for pulling nails and, of course, a ladder. Wear rubber-soled work shoes or boots for good traction and a hat for protection from the sun.

Don't even think about doing a roofing job if there are dormers which require difficult flashing work to prevent leaks, or if it's a steeply pitched roof, which is a dangerous place to work.

TIP BOX

Schedule the job in cool weather because working on a roof can be blisteringly hot during the summer.

TABLE

Pro Cost	DIY Cost	DIY Saving	% Saving	Pro Time	DIY Time
$820	$260	$560	68	12	25

REPLACING VINYL GUTTERS AND DOWNSPOUTS

Gutters and downspouts perform an important function: directing rainwater away from the house so it can't stain and damage the siding and seep into the soil around the foundation, causing a wet basement. Both are expensive to repair. By replacing old leaky gutters with a new vinyl system, you're practicing preventive medicine for your house, which will save you money in the long run.

A contractor will charge $500 to replace 100 linear feet of old gutter with a new vinyl system. If you're an experienced do-it-yourselfer, you can do the job for about $175, the cost of the components, and save a handsome 65 percent in the process.

These vinyl systems don't come cheap, but they snap together so they're easy to install. The components include ten sections of 10-foot-long gutter, six elbows, two downspouts, hanging straps, brackets and caulk. You'll use basic tools, and a chalk line makes the layout easy. Since you're working on a ladder, a cordless drill is handy. The vinyl sections can be cut with any saw, but a hacksaw works best.

When you shop for the components, you'll discover there are useful accessories that upgrade the system. For example, leaf screens are ideal in gutter sections where trees overhang, and self-cleaning down-spouts help eliminate clogging. The purchase of these accessories is not figured into the cost of this job, but you may decide the extra cost is worth the lower maintenance.

This is a weekend-long job and you'll need help from a friend with a ladder so there's someone to hold the gutter and downspout sections in place while you install them. Having someone on hand will save you countless trips up and down the ladder.

TIP BOX

For good drainage, install gutters with a half-inch slope every ten feet.

TABLE

Pro Cost	DIY Cost	DIY Saving	% Saving	Pro Time	DIY Time
$500	$175	$325	65	10	16

INSTALL A
MAILBOX ON A POST

The daily loading and unloading is a tough workout for a rural mailbox destined to take a beating from the weather. Its door hinges get sprung or break off, or the whole mailbox can get pushed out of shape by a passing snowplow. After years of use it's likely to need replacement.

To remove the old post and mailbox and replace it with a new unit is a do-able job for a homeowner with basic carpentry skills and tools. The price of mailboxes varies greatly—from a standard aluminum mailbox for $20, to a decorated, personalized fiberglass box for over a $100. A four-by-four pressure-treated wood or metal mailbox post costs an additional $15. The installation charge is about the same, so you will save about 30 percent whatever kind you choose. You can buy a post office–approved aluminum mailbox and post for $35 and install it yourself in an hour or hire a carpenter to do the job for about $50.

When shopping for a new mailbox and post, check to see how the box attaches to the post. If you choose a wooden post, you have to build a platform for the box to sit on; metal posts usually come with brackets.

You'll need a shovel and some basic tools that you probably have, but if you use a wooden post, rent or borrow a post hole digger (about $10) to make the hole. The hole should be deeper than the frost line, usually at least three feet, depending on the climate in your area. Hold the post upright with quick-setting, ready-mixed concrete. Unless your ground is unusually hard, a steel or aluminum post can generally be driven directly into the ground. The job should run about two hours from start to finish.

TIP BOX

Apply house numbers to the mailbox before installing it on the post, so it's easier to work on. To make sure the numbers are even and properly aligned, draw two layout lines above and below them. Place a pencil between the letters as a spacing gauge so the letters will be evenly spaced.

TABLE

Pro Cost	DIY Cost	DIY Saving	% Saving	Pro Time	DIY Time
$50	$35	$15	30	1	2

SEAL AN ASPHALT DRIVEWAY

A new topcoat of sealer on an asphalt driveway can make a dramatic difference. It's the kind of do-it-yourself project that you can't afford not to do, because it requires a minimum of work and inexpensive materials. A contractor charges $110 to seal a 1,000-square-foot driveway. For a few hours of work you can buy the materials for $35 and do it yourself, saving almost 70 percent.

Applying the sealer will take the least amount of time. The real work involves preparing the driveway surface if you want your job to last. Pull weeds that grow alongside the driveway or garden beds and rake the area so the driveway is neatly edged. Remove any grease or oil spots on the driveway with an asphalt cleaner. Fill small cracks with a mixture of plain sand and driveway sealer. First fill the crack with sealer, then apply the sand mix and tamp the area smooth. Large cracks and potholes should be filled with an asphalt patching compound. Pile the compound into the hole several inches higher than the surrounding driveway surface, then tamp down. Place a board over the patch and run your car wheel over the board to compress the patching compound.

An old push broom is a good applicator for spreading the sealer, or you can purchase an inexpensive spreader and throw it away after you are finished. Choose a dry day, without rain in the forecast, to seal the drive. Begin at the garage and work away from it, following the length of the driveway.

TIP BOX

Wear old clothes and shoes and be careful not to track any sealer indoors.

Move your car out of the garage before sealing the driveway!

TABLE

Pro Cost	DIY Cost	DIY Saving	% Saving	Pro Time	DIY Time
$110	$35	$75	68	1	3

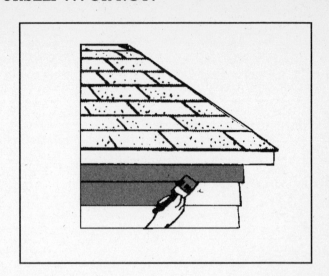

PAINT
A HOUSE

A homeowner can save big bucks by painting the exterior siding of a house, because the investment in materials is low. It's a labor-intensive job because of the many hours required to do the job right. For a typical 2,500-square-foot house you'll spend two weeks on the job and save 80 percent of what a contractor charges. A good part of the time you'll be preparing to paint; the actual painting requires much less time.

Our estimate covers the preparation work and application of 2 coats of paint on a one-story house with wood siding, 12 windows and 2 doors. The paint and materials cost $650. This includes 2 gallons of exterior primer for coating the worn and bare areas, 4 gallons alkyd exterior trim enamel and 15 gallons exterior flat paint. It also covers renting a 2,000 psi (pounds per square inch) pressure washer for three days ($75 a day) to clean the siding, and an additional $35 for incidentals like masking tape, drop cloths and mineral spirits. If you hired a painting contractor, you'd be charged about $3,000.

Patching and sanding the siding and trim is the key to a lasting paint job. If the exterior has holes or repair work required, be sure to do that before painting. You may have to budget more time if the house is in really bad shape. Take the time to protect shrubbery and plantings surrounding the house from paint drips with lightweight drop cloths or old sheets. Remove them as soon as painting is completed so they don't harm the plants.

TIP BOX

Buy a paint spinner to clean out brushes and rollers. Put a cleaned brush or roller in the spinner and twist the handle; it works like a kid's toy top and spins the brush or roller dry.

TABLE

Pro Cost	DIY Cost	DIY Saving	% Saving	Pro Time	DIY Time
$3,100	$650	$2,450	80	70	90

INSTALL A WEATHERVANE

A weathervane perched on top of your house is a real attention getter. Years ago merchants and farmers topped their roofs with vanes designed to identify their services or products so travelers and customers could identify them. Today weathervanes are used as decorative additions to homes, often identifying the owner's hobby or interest. A weathervane is also a handy indicator of the wind direction, a major factor determining weather conditions.

It's not difficult to install a weathervane if you don't mind working on a ladder on the roof. By doing it yourself, you'll save almost half of what a carpenter will charge. A good-quality weathervane made of copper or brass, with an iron mounting bracket that saddles the roof peak, sells for $150 or more. You'll see them offered for less, but a weathervane is a long-term investment so buy the best quality you can afford. To buy the same quality vane and have it installed will cost about $280.

When choosing a way to mount the vane on your roof, consider the two types of mounting brackets available: One fits over the existing roof shingles, and the other type mounts on the sidewall at the peak. Both types of mounting brackets are held in place with lag bolts. To install the bracket you need an electric drill and a wrench. You'll also need some roofing cement to seal any holes you make in the shingles.

TIP BOX

If the vane has moving parts, assemble it on the ground, then when the bracket is installed, attach the weathervane to it.

TABLE

Pro Cost	DIY Cost	DIY Saving	% Saving	Pro Time	DIY Time
$280	$150	$130	46	2	4

BUILD A REDWOOD DECK

With the addition of a deck, you can expand your living space to the outdoors while at the same time adding value to your house. You don't have to worry about rotting wood when you build a redwood deck, because it's long-lasting quality withstands years of the elements and everyday living.

Deck building is a good example of a labor-intensive job because it requires a week's worth of work for two of you. You'll pocket a 40 percent or better savings for your efforts. The cost of materials to build a single level 12-by-20-foot, 240-square-foot deck comes to about $1,600, which covers redwood lumber, cement for footings and galvanized nails and hardware. A contractor will charge $2,800 to do the job.

To help plan the deck take advantage of the design facilities at home centers where you buy the materials. Many of them offer a free computer design service which gives you a three-dimensional drawing of the deck design. To get the most out of these services make an accurate sketch of the exterior of the house, showing dimensions and door openings, outside stair locations, any obstructions and the height of the deck off the ground.

Check with your local building department to find out how deep to dig the footings and if there are building permit requirements affecting your lot. To build a deck you need sawhorses, a circular saw, an electric drill, basic carpentry tools, shovels and a wheelbarrow.

TIP BOX

Predrill the nail holes near the ends of the decking to prevent splitting. Use a decking nail in your electric drill to make the holes, instead of a standard drill bit.

TABLE

Pro Cost	DIY Cost	DIY Saving	% Saving	Pro Time	DIY Time
$2,800	$1,600	$1,200	42	52	80

REPLACE A GARAGE DOOR

Because of its size, a garage door makes a big impression as well as providing security for what's inside. You can replace an old one with a new 7-by-16-foot wooden double car door for $400 and install it yourself or hire a garage door company to do the job for about $700.

Despite the impressive 40 percent-plus savings, it's not a good job for a do-it-yourselfer unless you're experienced in construction. If the garage is out of square, you have to make adjustments so the opening is plumb and level. Depending on the condition of the old door's tracks, you may have to replace them and install new stop molding with vinyl seals on the jamb. If this is the case, leave this project to the professionals.

If you do decide to tackle this project, it's a two-person job because of the cumbersome size of the door. Have the door delivered, and no matter how experienced you are, follow the manufacturer's directions. Be very careful when working with the counterweight springs, because they're under substantial tension, especially when the door is down.

It's a weekend's worth of work because it involves various phases, and you'll need basic carpentry tools and a couple of adjustable wrenches.

TIP BOX

If the wood trim around the door needs a paint job, do it before installing the new door, when it's easiest to scrape and paint.

TABLE

Pro Cost	DIY Cost	DIY Saving	% Saving	Pro Time	DIY Time
$700	$400	$300	42	7	13

POWER WASH A DECK

The easiest way to clean a dirty deck is with a pressure washer, also called a power washer, which is hooked up to a hose and connected to a wandlike nozzle that you aim like a gun. When you pull the trigger, the washer shoots a forceful spray of water that blasts out dirt from the wood fibers. To rent a 1,000 psi (pounds per square inch) pressure washer costs about $50 a day. This size unit will fit in the trunk of most mid-sized or larger cars. There are larger, more powerful washers available with a selection of nozzle tips, but you need a pickup truck or van to transport them.

If you decide to hire out the job, when you ask for bids, you'll discover there's a wide range of prices, based on whether you're hiring a handyman or a cleaning service. For about $60 a handyman will pressure wash a 12-by-20-foot single-level deck, while a cleaning service— with a crew, equipment and trucks to support—may charge $110 or more. You will find cleaning services listed in the Yellow Pages under "Deck Cleaning" and in local newspaper classified ads under "Home Improvements."

If you do the job, it'll take about five hours and save you half of what a contractor charges.

To protect the deck after it's clean, apply a water sealer or repellent. The easiest way to apply the sealer is with a paint roller and pan. Begin at the house and work your way toward the outer edge and stairs. Use a paintbrush to coat the sides and ends of the decking where a roller can't reach.

TIP BOX

Replace nails that have worked loose, with galvanized, all-purpose deck screws driven close to the old ones. Fill the old hole with wood filler or a wooden plug.

TABLE

Pro Cost	DIY Cost	DIY Saving	% Saving	Pro Time	DIY Time
$110	$50	$60	55	4	5

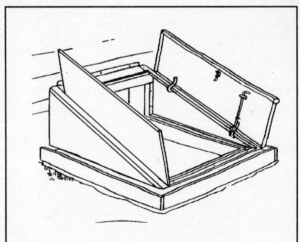

REPLACE A BASEMENT DOOR

One of the most convenient features of an older house is its basement door that opens wide so you can easily move bulky items like furniture and bicycles in and out. Over the years the original wooden door panels can become rotten and warped so they don't seal tightly. You can replace them easily with a steel basement door unit that comes in various sizes to fit different configurations. The unit includes a frame that you assemble, two doors and a torsion rod mechanism to open and close the doors. All the hardware for assembling the unit is included.

A contractor will charge up to $400 to remove an old wood bulkhead-type basement door and replace it with a new steel bulkhead-type door. You can buy a door unit and install it for $260, saving yourself 35 percent. You'll need to have these tools and materials on hand: hammer, nails, wrench, screwdriver, electric drill with masonry bit, tape measure and carpenter's level. It'll take about a day and a half.

The new door requires a level, sound surface. If the concrete or cinder block enclosure around the stairway opening is level and in good condition, it's a simple job to remove the old door and install the new unit. If the old door was installed on a sloping block or concrete wall, the sloping portion of the wall must be removed. If this is the case, plan to spend additional time and money if the concrete needs repair work or capping. It is worth the $25 to $30 a day rental fee to get an electric chipping hammer to break up the bad concrete or block walls.

TIP BOX

Seal the gap around the door frame, where it meets the exterior siding, with a good acrylic caulk.

TABLE

Pro Cost	DIY Cost	DIY Saving	% Saving	Pro Time	DIY Time
$400	$260	$140	35	5	12

CHAPTER
8

INSTALL A
SPRINKLER SYSTEM

The two most common mistakes that homeowners make tending their lawn are under- and over-watering it. The lawn either dries out or drowns. By installing an automatic, below-the-ground lawn sprinkling system you can prevent these problems and maintain a healthy lawn throughout the year.

Take a trip to your local home and garden center to see the sprinkler systems that are designed for do-it-yourself installation. The systems are made up of modular components, like control valves and sprinkler heads, that are connected together with plastic piping. For an average-sized lot installing one of these systems is a do-able project for a homeowner.

Even as a do-it-yourself project, it's an expensive improvement. To install a sprinkling system for a 4,000-square-foot lawn, the components will cost $740. A landscaper will charge $2,370 to do the job. If you decide to tackle the job, plan on spending a full week of strenuous work and saving almost 70 percent for your labor. To save time and prevent

some sore back muscles digging trenches for the pipes, rent a portable gas-powered trencher. It digs a four-inch-deep trench that is one inch wide, and rents for about $60 a day.

TIP BOX

Read the "Planning Guide," which most manufacturers provide, for the sprinkler system and study it thoroughly so you know what's involved. Avoid running pipes beneath driveways or walkways.

TABLE

Pro Cost	DIY Cost	DIY Saving	% Saving	Pro Time	DIY Time
$2,370	$740	$1,630	68	41	55

LAY A
BRICK PATIO

The long-lasting quality and traditional appeal of a brick patio makes it a worthwhile addition to any home or landscape. Laying one is an ambitious project, but certainly within the scope of a do-it-yourselfer. And it's an enticing project because you can save 75 percent of what a contractor charges if you do it yourself. For about $260 worth of materials you can lay a 120-square-foot red brick patio, which is considerably less than the $1,120 a contractor charges.

To lay a 10-by-12-foot patio you need 500 bricks and at least 1 cubic yard of sand. Since these materials are heavy and cumbersome, have them delivered. Bricks look best laid in a pattern, and a basket weave is a popular design for a patio. A bricklayer can set this pattern freehand but you will be better off using plastic grid trays, which hold eight bricks in a basket weave pattern. The trays also help combat the growth of weeds, since they act as a ground cover.

The bulk of the work is the excavation. Bricks are $2\frac{1}{4}$ inches thick and should be set in at least 2 inches of sand, so you have to remove about 5 inches of soil. If the area is covered by a healthy lawn, consider saving the sod to lay somewhere else. To remove a large stretch of lawn, for about $60 a day, rent a sod cutter which is a gas-propelled machine that cuts the sod into strips.

This is a week's worth of work so pace yourself and plan the work accordingly.

TIP BOX

To plan the overall design and layout of the patio, use graph paper or a computer with a house design program.

| TABLE | | | | | |
Pro Cost	DIY Cost	DIY Saving	% Saving	Pro Time	DIY Time
$1,120	$260	$860	75	25	38

LAYING SOD

A plush green lawn surrounding a just built house goes a long way to establish the residence in its new surrounding. In another way an old house is granted a new lease on life when a carpet of sod is laid, replacing a worn and weed-filled yard.

To lay sod requires some backbreaking work, but you'll be rewarded for your labor with more than a 70 percent savings over the cost of hiring a landscaper.

The cost comparison for this project is based on an average-sized lawn requiring 150 square yards of sod, with a minimum of soil preparation and no excavation. You can expect to pay about $240 for the sod and about $850 to have a landscaper do the job. So doing it yourself is a big money saver. Sod prices do fluctuate so call a local sod farm or nursery to get the current cost depending on weather conditions and the area where you live. A price of $1.40 a square yard for sod was used to estimate the cost of this project.

The most time-consuming part of the job is preparing the soil. The actual laying of the sod is the fun part. If you have to dig up and remove an old lawn, or if the ground is rocky, the job becomes more time- and labor-intensive. Unless you have a pickup truck, it's a good idea to have the sod delivered, which costs about $50. Plan to lay the sod as soon as it arrives, so it doesn't dry out. You'll need a wheelbarrow, garden rakes, hoses and a sprinkler. Rent or borrow a lawn roller.

If you're lucky, you'll schedule laying the sod for a gray day with clouds overhead and mild temperatures. And before and after the sod is laid, a slow, soaking rain will fall, easing the roots into the soil.

TIP BOX

Begin laying sod along a sidewalk or driveway so you can work your way out from a straight edge. Use an old kitchen knife to cut it to size.

TABLE

Pro Cost	DIY Cost	DIY Saving	% Saving	Pro Time	DIY Time
$850	$240	$610	70	18	30

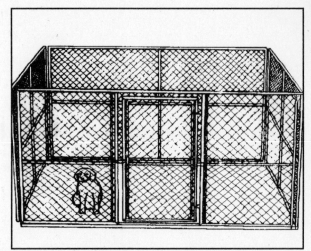

BUILD A DOG KENNEL

When the family pet needs a place to call his or her own outside the house, build a chain-link kennel. It's a do-able project that even a not-so-handy homeowner can handle. The materials needed to build a 10-by-15-foot enclosure with a gate that is 6 feet high cost about $365. A fencing contractor will charge about $600 to build a kennel, so you'll save almost 40 percent for your effort. You'll spend two long days of work from start to finish.

Large home centers and fence companies sell the materials needed, which include fencing fabric, posts, mounting hardware and a gate. You can also buy a kennel kit which contains all the components.

Check with your local building department to see if there's a preferred way to install the posts. Typical installation is either putting them in cement or using post anchors. The cost is about the same for either system. Rent a post hole digger if you use cement to anchor the posts. When using anchors, rent a post driver. To stretch the chain fabric from post to post, rent a chain fabric stretcher, which runs about $25 a day.

TIP BOX

The best location for a kennel is on dry level ground that is shaded from the sun.

TABLE

Pro Cost	DIY Cost	DIY Saving	% Saving	Pro Time	DIY Time
$590	$365	$225	38	8	15

BUILD A
120-FOOT PICKET FENCE WITH GATE

When it comes to adding curb appeal to a house, a picket fence is a good choice. Its traditional look adds charm and warmth to just about any house while creating a secure environment around it. Fence building is not for the faint of heart, because it requires many hours of muscle-straining, back-bending work. You're rewarded, however, with a hefty 60 percent savings for your labor. To build a 120-foot cedar or pressure-treated wood picket fence with a gate, a fence contractor will charge $860. For $350 you can buy the fencing, posts and cement and build it yourself.

To build a fence you'll need basic carpentry tools, and a circular saw will make the job easier to complete. The fencing comes in 8-foot prefabricated sections which are connected at posts set in cement. To help expedite digging all the post holes, it's a good idea to rent a post hole digger, which costs less than $10 a day.

This is a time-consuming project so expect to spend at least two long weekends of work completing the job.

When you build a fence, it's important to make certain you know the exact location of your property line so you don't build on your neighbor's land. Find the location on a survey of the property, and if you're uncertain, hire a surveyor to stake it out. A misplaced fence will be a major problem when either you or your neighbor decide to sell your property. Also check with the local building department to ask if there are any restrictions. To know the location of buried cables or wires call the Miss Utility program in your area before digging.

TIP BOX

Finish the fence with stain instead of paint and you will have much less maintenance.

TABLE

Pro Cost	DIY Cost	DIY Saving	% Saving	Pro Time	DIY Time
$860	$350	$510	60	13	35

INSTALL A FLAGPOLE

A sturdy flagpole is a stately yard ornament, made more attractive when it's flying Old Glory. It's a handsome addition that's enjoyed by everyone who sees it—homeowners, neighbors and passersby. If you're a do-it-yourselfer, you can buy a flagpole kit and install it in ready-mixed concrete. It's a full day's work because of the digging and installation required. The kit contains a sectional, anodized aluminum, 25-foot flagpole with ball top, pulley, foundation tube and flashing collar. You can buy the kit for $215 and install it, saving 34 percent of the contractor's charge of $325.

Before digging a hole in your yard, make a call to your local building department. Check to see if a permit is required to erect a flagpole and find out exactly how deep you have to dig the footing; it varies depending on the depth of the frost line in your area. Don't dig any holes in your yard without knowing the location of buried wires or cables. To find out the location, call the Miss Utility program in your area.

TIP BOX

The bigger the better, when it comes to flags. A 4-by-6-foot or 5-by-8-foot flag will be just the right size.

TABLE

Pro Cost	DIY Cost	DIY Saving	% Saving	Pro Time	DIY Time
$325	$215	$110	34	4	8

EDGE A GARDEN BED

You can use an edging tool with a half-moon blade to dig a trench around garden beds or make the transition from lawn to garden more pronounced by installing a permanent edging material. In home and garden centers you'll find a selection of precast edging materials to lay in sand. These can be bricks or precast concrete ornamental systems that define the borders of a garden bed while keeping weeds and grass from encroaching into the flowers. This project is ideal for a do-it-yourselfer because the investment in tools and materials is low and the skills required are easy to learn since they're repetitive. You'll save more than half of what a landscaper will charge.

The materials needed to lay 50 feet of border with precast edging cost $55, compared with the $120 a landscaper will charge for the labor and material. The materials include 25 sections of 24-inch-long edging and a few bags of sand. Since this material is heavy, it's a good idea to have it delivered unless you have a van or truck.

From start to finish the job will take about four hours of working the soil, pouring the sand, leveling it and installing the edging material. The only gardening tools and equipment you'll need are a shovel, a spade or an edging tool and a container to hold the soil you remove.

TIP BOX

For good-looking results set the edging materials at the same height or just above the level of the plant bed. If the ground is uneven, you'll have to adjust the height of the edging.

TABLE

Pro Cost	DIY Cost	DIY Saving	% Saving	Pro Time	DIY Time
$120	$55	$65	54	2	4

INSTALL A STONE GARDEN PATH

A stepping stone through a yard or garden is a sound surface for good footing and an attractive addition to the landscape. The project is labor-intensive because it involves excavating the path and handling heavy stones. By doing it yourself, you'll save more than half of what a landscaper charges. The savings are well earned because you'll spend at least two days of work. The most difficult work is excavating the path, because you have to dig down 4 inches to allow for a 2-inch sand base and the depth of the stone.

The stone and sand for a 2-foot-wide-by-20-foot-long flagstone walkway will cost $140. A landscaper will do the job for $400. Lay out the path with strings and stakes and then remove the dirt within the outline. If the walk runs through a grassy area, remove the sod and use it to patch bare spots. Then spread and grade the sand base so it is smooth and level. The final step is choosing and laying down pieces of flagstone so they fit together like a puzzle. When they're in place, spread sand over the stones, sweeping it in between the cracks.

If the walkway runs over hard, compacted ground or around a tree with a large surface root system, consider hiring a landscape contractor, who has the equipment and expertise to get the job done without damaging the tree.

TABLE

Pro Cost	DIY Cost	DIY Saving	% Saving	Pro Time	DIY Time
$400	$140	$260	65	11	18

BUILD A KID'S GYM SET

A play center in the backyard offers hours of fun and exercise for kids. These outdoor gym sets are available in various configurations so they can be adapted and arranged to fit a particular site. As kids grow older and stronger, more challenging components can be added to the center. A typical version is constructed with wooden supports and incorporates a swing, play fort, climbing rope, slide, pole and ladder.

A handy homeowner with basic carpentry skills can buy a precut kit and assemble the components, because all the necessary hardware and instructions are included. The kit costs $450 and takes a good ten hours of work to assemble. Another choice is to spend $650 to have the materials delivered and assembled on site. You'll save about a third by supplying a long day of labor.

For an experienced home carpenter there's a third option: designing and building a gym set from scratch.

Some of the play systems are anchored into the ground with stakes or cement, and others are designed to be freestanding. The components are sold ready-to-assemble, with timbers that are precut, with most of the major holes drilled. To assemble the system you need a pair of pliers and an adjustable wrench. A socket wrench set is particularly handy since there are lots of nuts and bolts to tighten.

You'll find these gym set kits sold in various places, including lumberyards, home and garden centers and specialty stores.

Before buying one, check with your local building department to see if there are any zoning requirements, such as height restrictions, to consider. Also check that you know where your property line runs so that your gym set is built entirely on your land.

TIP BOX

Unless you have a pickup truck or van, have the components delivered to the area where they'll be used, because they're heavy and cumbersome to move.

TABLE

Pro Cost	DIY Cost	DIY Saving	% Saving	Pro Time	DIY Time
$650	$450	$200	31	5	10

SOURCES

CELLAR DOOR

The Bilco Co., P. O. Box 123, New Haven, CT 06505, 203/943-6363

CEMENT BOARD

Durock by United States Gypsum, P. O. Box 806278, Chicago, IL 60680-4142, 1-800-347-1345

CENTRAL VACUUM SYSTEM

Electrolux, 2300 Windy Ridge Pky., Suite 900, Marietta, GA 30067, 800/243-5893

NuTone Inc., Madison and Red Bank Roads, Cincinnati, OH 45227, 513/527-5100

CORNICE BOARD KIT

Plaid Enterprises, 1649 International Blvd., P. O. Box 7600, Norcross, GA 30091-7600, 404/923-8200

FULL ACCESS FOLDING DOOR HARDWARE

L. E. Johnson Products, Inc., 2100 Sterling Ave., Elkhart, IN 46516, 219/293-5664

IRONING CENTER

NuTone Inc., Madison and Red Bank Roads, Cincinnati, OH 45227, 513/527-5100

MISS UTILITY PROGRAM

800/555-1212

PLANK CEILING SYSTEM

Plank Ceilings by Armstrong World Industries, 313 W. Liberty St., P. O.
   Box 3001, Lancaster, PA 17604-3001, 717/397-0611

PLASTER WASHERS

Charles St. Supply Co., 54 Charles St., Boston, MA 02114, 617/367-9046

POLYSTYRENE MOLDING

Cantebury Molding by ABTco., Inc., 3250 W. Big Beaver Rd., Suite 200,
   Troy, MI 48084, 800/521-4250

Finishing Touches by Armstrong World Industries, 313 W. Liberty St.,
   P. O. Box 3001, Lancaster, PA 17604-3001, 717/397-0611

PRIMER-SEALER STAIN KILLER

B-I-N by Zinsser Products, 39 Belmont Dr., Somerset, NJ 08875-1285,
   908/469-8100

RECYCLED WALLBOARD

FiberBond by Louisiana-Pacific, P. O. Box 10266, Portland OR 97210-9936,
   800/299-0028

TEXTURED PAINT REMOVER

Texture-Off by Zinsser Products, 39 Belmont Dr., Somerset, NJ 08875-1285,
   908/469-8100

WINDOW JAMB LINER KIT

Window Fixer Replacement Channels by Quaker City Manufacturing
   Co., 701 Chester Pike, Sharon Hill, PA 19079, 215/586-4770

ABOUT THE AUTHORS

Katie and Gene Hamilton are the authors of the weekly syndicated newspaper column "Do-It-Yourself . . . or Not?" as well as ten home improvement and woodworking books, including *Fix It Fast, Fix It Right* and *How to Be Your Own Contractor*. They have contributed to a number of national magazines and are the creators of HouseNet BBS, a computer on-line service about home improvements, available on the Internet (www.housenet.com) and on America Online.